Essential
Japanese Grammar

By
EVERETT F. BLEILER

DOVER PUBLICATIONS, INC.
NEW YORK

Published in Canada by General Publishing Company, Limited, 30 Lesmill Road, Don Mills, Toronto, Ontario.
Published in the United Kingdom by Constable and Company, Limited, 10 Orange Street, London WC 2.

Essential Japanese Grammer is a new work, first published by Dover Publications, Inc., in 1963.

Standard Book Number: 486-21027-8
Library of Congress Catalog Card Number: 63-17899

Manufactured in the United States of America

Dover Publications, Inc.
180 Varick Street
New York, N. Y. 10014

Table of Contents

3

Page

How to Use this Booklet

Essential Japanese Grammar assumes that you will be spending a limited number of hours studying Japanese grammar and that your objective is simple everyday communication. It is offered not as a condensed outline of all aspects of Japanese grammar, but as a series of aids which will enable you to use more effectively and with greater versatility phrases and vocabulary that you have previously learned. It will familiarize you with the more common structure and patterns of the language.

If this is your first introduction to Japanese grammar, the following suggestions may be helpful.

1. Don't approach *Essential Japanese Grammar* until you have mastered many useful phrases and expressions such as you will find in any good phrase book or the *Listen and Learn* course.

2. Start at the beginning of this book and read through it. Look up unfamiliar or confusing grammatical terms in the short glossary in the rear. Don't be concerned if sections are not immediately clear to you. On second or third reading they will make better sense. What may appear discouragingly difficult at first will become understandable as your studies progress. As you use the language and hear it spoken, many aspects of Japanese grammar will begin to form recognizable patterns.

3. Go back to *Essential Japanese Grammar* periodically. Sections which seem difficult or of doubtful benefit to you now, may prove extremely helpful later.

4. For the most part, *Essential Japanese Grammar* is presented in a logical order, especially for the major divisions of grammar, and you will do best if you follow its sequence in your studies. However, the author is aware that some students learn best when they study to answer their immediate questions and needs (e.g. how to form the comparative; the conjugation of the verb *to be*, etc.).   If you prefer to work in this manner, study entire sections rather than isolated parts.

Introductory Material

Introduction to the Japanese Language

Japanese, unlike the other foreign languages that you are likely to have studied, is not a member of the Indo-European family, and is not related to English. Nor is it related to Chinese, even though it has borrowed a large vocabulary from Chinese. It is pretty much a language by itself, although it may be related to Korean, and some philologists believe that in the far distant past it had a common ancestor with certain Central Asiatic languages that are called Altaic. But these possible relationships are remote, and can be appreciated only by comparative philologists.

As a result of this linguistic distance from English, Japanese grammar is very different from English grammar. This difference is not just a question of different forms and endings, as is often the case between English and German or French or Spanish or Russian; it is frequently a question of a different classification of human experience. You must be prepared when you study Japanese grammar to suspend your ideas of what the parts of speech are and how they are used, what a sentence is and how it is constructed, how ideas are expressed and how variations on these ideas are indicated. As you read through this manual, do not limit yourself to memorizing the construction of forms and idea-equations between English and Japanese. Try also to understand the psychology of language which lies behind this often very different way of talking about experience. You will find this very broadening, for you soon learn that many of the standards that you hold (consciously or unconsciously) about language are not necessary. You will be surprised to discover that many of the concepts which we consider indispensable to "sense" can be stripped away and discarded, with no real loss to meaning.

In some ways Japanese is simpler than English, and in other

ways it is more complex.   It can be extremely simple in its expression of basic ideas, yet very elaborate in expressing the speaker's feeling about the ideas.   The conversational situation affects expression more than it does in English, and forms of courtesy enter much more than they do in European languages.   Japanese is extremely regular in its grammatical forms; the exceptions to the grammatical rules of formation can be counted on your fingers.   On the other hand, syntax and sentence structure can become very complex, and idioms are numerous.

This manual does not provide a complete coverage of Japanese grammar, but has been limited to constructions which are indispensable to either comprehension or ordinary simple speech. We have omitted many verb forms that you probably would not hear very often, and we have presented a very small number of special constructions and idioms.   Where there is a choice among several ways of expressing an idea—which is often the case in Japanese—we have tried to create a balance between the most commonly used Japanese forms and the forms that are easiest for an American to master.   This is not baby Japanese, however, or kitchen Japanese, or any other pidgin language that has grown up among foreigners who do not care to learn correct Japanese.   It is just the simpler, basic aspect of modern colloquial Japanese. While you may find a more complex Japanese (with, at times, different forms and constructions than we give) in books, periodicals, and newspapers, this book teaches the standard colloquial Japanese that is understood anywhere in Japan.

As we have already said, Japanese grammar does not always parallel English grammar, and it would be a distortion to present Japanese in terms of English forms or ideas.   It would be equally inadvisable to present it in the system that native Japanese grammarians follow, or in the technical analysis of a comparative philologist.   Instead, we have tried to present a descriptive grammar that can be easily followed by an English speaker, yet does not depart from the spirit of the language.   The English terminology for Japanese grammar, unfortunately, has not yet been standardized, so that constructions may be called by many different names according to the grammar book that one uses. Our approach to this problem has been eclectic: we have selected the term that seems to fit the situation best and seems to be the most meaningful to an English speaker. We have often mentioned other terminologies, however, so that you will not be at a loss if you continue on to more advanced grammars.

Notation

Beneath each Japanese sentence we have supplied a literal word-for-word translation of the sentence. In some cases this can be only approximate, since there is no real word-for-word correspondence between the two languages, but it will still indicate to you the grammatical processes involved and the psychology of language behind the grammar and syntax.

To keep the parallelism exact, we have often hyphenated the English literal translation, so that you can identify correspondences. The Japanese word *wa*, for example, we have translated literally as "as-for," so that by the English you can understand that a single word is involved in Japanese. In most cases English is more verbose than Japanese, and it is only rarely that two Japanese words must be translated by a single English word. Such a case is the Japanese sequence *no de*, which we translate as "since" or "because." To retain the word-for-word parallelism, we have inserted a long dash in the English. You need not worry about this, since it occurs in only two or three places.

Grammatical processes occur in Japanese for which there are no English translations. In such cases we have made use of the following arbitrary English abbreviations to indicate the Japanese meaning:

> *sj* (which is normally placed under the Japanese word *ga* in our literal translation) indicates that the preceding word is the subject of the clause or sentence.
>
> *oj* (which is normally placed under the Japanese word *o* in our literal translation) indicates the preceding word is the direct object of the verb.

qu (which is normally placed under the Japanese word *ka* in our literal translation) is equivalent to a question mark. It indicates that the sentence is a question.

hon indicates that something has been inserted into a sentence or has been added to a word to express respect. It has no literal lexical meaning, but is part of the linguistic etiquette of the language. For example, the word *tegami* would normally be translated as "letter"; the word *otegami*, however, also means "letter," but the prefix *o-* indicates a certain feeling of courtesy or respect which we cannot translate into English (though in cartoon-strip Japanese-English this would be translated as "your honorable letter"). To indicate the presence of this honorific (for a full discussion see page 116), we translate *otegami* literally as "*hon*-letter," and in the colloquial English translation as simply "letter."

The colloquial English translation that appears below the literal translation is somewhat arbitrary in many cases, since it reflects what might be expected in a normal conversational situation. In most cases other translations could be equally valid. You will appreciate this point after you have worked through this grammar.

Basic Japanese

You may not have the time to work through this series of grammatical aids. For an acquaintance with the absolute minimum of Japanese grammar, we suggest that you read the following sections:

With a command of this material you should be able to express most simple statements, even though you will not be able to express any complexity of thought. You should also be able to understand the grammatical situations in most simple statements that may be made to you. We advise you, however, to advance beyond these sections, if possible. Japanese grammar, though different from your past experience, is not really difficult, and a knowledge of basic forms and concepts will greatly enlarge your ability to understand and to express yourself, and will make your travel more pleasant.

General Information

In this section we shall anticipate the more detailed explanations that follow in the remainder of this book, and shall give you a brief summary of important points of Japanese grammar that are likely to be strange to you. Bear these points in mind as you work through the rest of these hints, and you will probably be able to understand the general structure of Japanese better and to follow the speech patterns in the sentences and phrases that we give as examples.

1. There are no words corresponding to the English words a, an, or the.

2. Nouns do not have special plural forms; they remain the same whether they indicate one object or many. The Japanese word *to*, for example, can mean a door, the door, doors, or the doors.

3. Pronouns are usually omitted if they can be understood from the context. But they can be used for emphasis, or when they are needed to make the meaning clear.

Ex.   Ikaga desu ka?   Genki desu.
        [how is *qu*]   [good-health is]
        How are you?   I am fine, thank you.

        Kare wa, hon ga kaitai?
        [he as-for book *sj* buying-wishing *qu*]
        Does he want to buy a book?

4. Verbs do not have special forms to indicate person or number. Each tense has only one form, which is used no matter what the subject is. *yomu* (to read), for example, could be the form used to translate the word "read" in any of these situations: I read, you read, he reads, we read, they read, the man reads, and so on.

5. True Japanese adjectives are closely related to verbs, and take endings according to their tense and mood. You use the dictionary form when an adjective modifies a noun.

6. There are no cases for nouns or pronouns. Relationships between the words of a sentence are indicated by little words called particles or postpositions, which are placed *after* the word they control. The most common are: *ga*, which usually indicates the subject of a clause; *wa*, which can be translated as "as-for" and often indicates the subject of a clause; *o*, which follows the direct object; *no*, which means "of" in most of the English senses of the word, and indicates possession; and *ka*, which indicates a question.

Ex.   Kisha ga kimasu.   Kyō wa yoi tenki desu.
        [train *sj* comes]   [today as-for good weather is]
        The train comes.   The weather is fine today.

        Watakushi wa sore o mimasu. Anata wa gakusei desu ka?
        [I as-for that *oj* see]   [you as-for student is *qu*]
        I see it.   Are you a student?

7. The frequent endings -*masu*, -*mashita*, and -*mashō* are verb endings. They indicate, respectively, the present tense, the past tense, and a peculiarly Japanese mode which is usually translated by using the word "probably" in the sentence. The ending -*masen* indicates a present negative verb; -*masen deshita* a past tense negative; and -*masen deshō* indicates a negative tense involving probability—"probably does not," etc. All of these are polite forms and are the forms that you are most likely to meet in ordinary conversation.

8. The common ending -*te* usually indicates a verb participle, which can be translated into English in most cases by a present participle (-ing): *kite*, coming; *aruite*, walking; *shite*, doing.

9. Basic word order is subject—object—verb. Japanese is somewhat rigid with respect to word order, and verbs must come last.

> Ex.   Watakushi wa shimbun o yonde imasu.
> [I as-for newspaper *oj* reading am]
> As for me, I'm reading a newspaper.

10. Conjunctions come at the end of the clause they govern.

11. Subordinate clauses must come first in the sentence. You must say: If I see him, I will pay him. You cannot say: I will pay him if I see him.

Do not be disturbed or discouraged if you do not understand these situations completely or if you do not understand why certain forms have been made or used. Simply accept them for what they are. We have provided this forewarning to Japanese grammar only to give you orientation before you consider reasons and details later. Language study is all too often a spiderweb of interrelated problems, in which it is not always possible to follow one strand without disturbing other strands, and invoking other equally complex situations. A fragment of background knowledge can often make your learning task much easier.

The Language of Courtesy (Introductory)

Japanese is very rich in special forms which indicate shades of courtesy, respect, and formality that often are impossible to express in English. These forms originally demonstrated the amount of social respect or awe that the speaker felt toward the person he was addressing or toward a third party. This concept of a language of respect (which has certainly had less complex parallels in the Western world) originally arose in the highly stratified society of Imperial China, where language was often a means of retaining or enhancing one's own position by insulting inferiors and fawning upon superiors. These concepts then moved to Japan. Even today, although the social stratification that gave birth to them has been broken, these archaic forms have been frozen in place and are still customarily used, though at times to a lesser degree.

For the purpose of this brief outline of grammar we may say that there are four levels of language etiquette—although the actual number might be argued. These are (1) rude, which you might use toward inferiors or as an insult; (2) abrupt-neutral, which in some constructions is neutral in tone, and in other situations is somewhat abrupt to use toward an equal; (3) normal-polite, which you would use to your equals and perhaps your superiors; (4) very polite, which you would use to superiors. In this grammar we have restricted ourselves to abrupt-neutral (2) and normal-polite (3), which are the forms you will hear in everyday life. We have also included a few very polite forms which seem to be moving down toward normal-polite acceptance.

Since it is better if you err on the side of politeness rather than of rudeness, you will probably be safest if you use the polite forms that we stress in this series of grammatical aids. You should also use the abrupt-neutral forms in the special grammatical situations that we shall indicate. After you have spent some time in Japan and have learned the proper social situations, you can enlarge your speech level with more safety.

Nouns

Japanese nouns have only one form, which is not changed to indicate number, gender, or the role that the noun plays within the sentence. The same form is used under all circumstances. This form also includes within itself the ideas of the English "the" and "a" (or "an"), which do not exist separately in Japanese.

jidōsha an automobile, the automobile, the automobiles, automobiles

kisha a train, the train, the trains, trains

dempō a telegram, the telegram, the telegrams, telegrams

This will probably seem very imprecise to you, and you may wonder how you are going to express your thoughts. You will soon discover that you can get along perfectly well without special plural forms, just as you do with such English words as sheep, fish, quail, or deer.

In most cases, the number of things that you are talking about will be clear from context. Where it is necessary to be specific, you can always use numbers or words indicating quantity, just as we do with the English nouns that have no separate plural form. (For the way that you use numbers with nouns, which is quite different from English, see page 124.)

takusan no jidōsha
[quantity of auto]
many automobiles

Personal Pronouns

In modern colloquial Japanese the personal pronouns are usually omitted if the meaning of the sentence is clear without them, just as is the case in Spanish or Italian.

Ikaga desu ka?   Genki desu.
[how are *qu*]   [fine-health is]
How are you?   I am fine.

When it is necessary to express a pronoun, either for emphasis or for clearness, use the words in this table:

watakushi	I, me	watakushitachi*	we, us
anata	you (SING.)	anatatachi*	you (PL.)
kare	he, him	karera	they, them (MASC.)
kanojo	she, her	kanojotachi	they, them (FEM.)

In addition to these normal-polite forms, Japanese is very rich in other words which convey a great variety of shades of familiarity, politeness, and formality. Most of these forms are beyond the scope of this manual, but you should be aware of two other personal pronouns which are very commonly used:

boku   I, me   kimi   you

These words are less courteous and less formal than *watakushi* and *anata*, and they are used in conversation between intimates and members of some social groups, such as students.

Like nouns, pronouns do not change their forms according to their use within a sentence. Thus, as the tables show, *watakushi* can mean I or me, *boku* can mean I or me, and so on.

* You will also hear the forms *watakushidomo* for we and *anatagata* for you (PL.).

We can anticipate the discussion of possessives (see page 24) to say that the pronominal adjectives are formed entirely regularly and simply by placing the word *no* after the pronoun in question.

watakushi no	my	watakushitachi no	our
anata no	your	anatatachi no	your (PL.)
kare no	his	karera no	their (MASC.)
kanojo no	her	kanojotachi no	their (FEM.)
		boku no	my
		kimi no	your

Sentences:

Watakushi no namae wa Kido desu.
[I of name as-for Kido is]
My name is Kido.

Sore ga watakushi no desu.
[that *sj* I of is]
That is mine.

Anata wa sensei desu ka?
[you as-for teacher are *qu*]
Are you a teacher?

Iie. Watakushi wa gakusei desu.
[no. I as-for student am]
No, I am a student.

Kimi to boku wa dokyūsei desu.
[you and I as-for classmates are]
You and I are classmates.

Karera wa watakushitachi o matte imasu.
[they as-for we *oj* waiting are]
They are waiting for us.

The impersonal pronoun it, in such expressions as, "It is raining," "It is Sunday," is not translated into Japanese.

Ame ga futte imasu.
[rain *sj* falling is]
It is raining.

Nichiyō desu.
[Sunday is]
It is Sunday.

Using Nouns and Pronouns in Sentences

Japanese, like English, has the concepts of subject, of sentences, direct objects, and indirect objects, but it expresses these concepts in a different manner.

In English we show the relationships between the words of a sentence mostly by word order: "The policeman chased the burglar" is obviously quite different in meaning from "The burglar chased the policeman." Only in the pronouns, in English, do we have different forms or endings to show the function of a word in a sentence: I, me, my, he, him, his, we, our, and so on.

In Japanese, however, the sentence function of nouns and pronouns is shown by additional words that are placed immediately after the noun or pronoun. (Word order, which is also extremely important, will be considered later: page 118.) These words, which are called particles or postpositions, might by a stretch of the imagination be considered as acting in the same way as the case endings that you learned if you studied German or Latin, although in Japanese these particles never vary, but always remain the same.

The three most important of these signposts within a sentence are *ga, wa,* and *o.*

ga usually indicates the grammatical subject of the sentence or clause in which it appears. We specify grammatical subject because the Japanese grammatical subject is very often not the logical subject in the English translation. *ga* indicates that the immediately preceding noun or pronoun is the subject, and we indicate it in our literal translation by the symbol *sj.*
Sentences:

> Ame ga harete, hi ga tette imasu.
> [rain *sj* ceasing, sun *sj* shining is]
> It has stopped raining, and the sun is shining.

Atama ga itaimasu.	Yamazaki san ga kuru.
[head *sj* pains]	[Yamazaki Mr. *sj* comes]
I have a headache.	Mr. Yamazaki comes.

wa (spelled *ha* in the Japanese syllabary) indicates that the material which it immediately follows is to be set apart from the grammatical basis of the Japanese sentence. A rough English translation that will fit it in most situations is "as-for."

> Kyō wa umi ga taihen kirei desu.
> [today as-for sea *sj* very beautiful is]
> Today the sea is very beautiful.

> Boku wa ashita ongakkai ni yukimasu.
> [I as-for tomorrow concert to go]
> As for me, tomorrow I shall go to the concert. I shall go to the concert tomorrow.

As you may have observed in the sentences above, *wa* often indicates material that is the subject of the English translation.

> Anata wa eigo ga dekimasu ka?
> [you as-for English-language *sj* able *qu*]
> Do you speak English?

You may be puzzled about when you should use *ga* to indicate the subject, and when you should use *wa*. Actually, this involves a very subtle distinction in Japanese thought, and is very difficult for a foreigner to master. This point is beyond the scope of these grammatical notes. We can say, however, that *wa* on the whole is best translated by placing emphasis on the predicate of the sentence, and *ga* by placing emphasis on the subject.

> Kare wa hikōki de kimasu.
> [he as-for airplane by comes]
> He is coming by airplane. (emphasis on coming by airplane)

> Kare ga hikōki de kimasu.
> [he *sj* airplane by comes]
> He is coming by airplane. (emphasis upon he)

It is possible for us to make these distinctions in English, but we are much less concerned with them than is Japanese.

o (sometimes transliterated *wo*, and spelled *wo* in the Japanese *kana* writing) indicates that the preceding word is the direct object of the verb. It is often used with verbs of motion that English would consider incapable of taking a direct object:

> Omiyage o kaimashita.
> [souvenirs *oj* bought]
> I (or you, or he, etc.) bought some souvenirs.
>
> Kōbe o tachimashita.
> [Kōbe *oj* left]
> We (or I, or you, or he, etc.) left Kōbe.

It is very important that you understand how these postpositions are used, since they are the cement which bonds together the parts of a Japanese sentence. They cannot be omitted in a grammatically correct sentence, if nouns or pronouns are present.* You must indicate the subject of a clause by either *ga* or *wa*, and you must indicate the direct object, if there is one, by *o*.

The two common particles that are used to form questions may also be mentioned here. These are *ka* and *ne*.

ka is normally placed at the end of a question, and is equivalent to an English question mark. *ne*, which is also placed at the end of the sentence, is equivalent to the French "n'est-ce pas" or German "nicht wahr" or English "isn't it?" *ne* often has the feeling of an exclamation.

> Kore wa nan desu ka?
> [this as-for what is *qu*]
> As for this, what is it?   What is this?

---

* In very colloquial speech, *wa* (and the other postpositions to a lesser extent) are occasionally omitted. But it is better if you avoid this, and use postpositions wherever they are called for.

Rikōna kodomo desu ne?
[intelligent child is isn't-it]
It's an intelligent child, isn't it?   What an intelligent child!

Kare wa amerika-jin desu ne?
[he as-for America-man is isn't-he]
He is an American, isn't he?

Particles Equivalent to Prepositions, Adverbs, Conjunctions

Besides the three basic particles of sentence structure (*ga, wa,* and *o*) and the two particles that indicate questions (*ka* and *ne*), Japanese has a very wide range of words that are equivalent in function to the English prepositions, adverbs, and conjunctions. All of these particles are placed after the word they modify, and for this reason are called *post*positions, instead of *pre*positions. We shall discuss only the most important of these secondary particles here: *no, to, ya, kara, made, ni, e, de,* and *mo*.

no corresponds in many ways to the English preposition "of." It can indicate:*

(1) possession, ownership, attribution.

Kore ga boku no shashinki desu.
[this *sj* I of camera is]
This is my camera.

(2) material.

Ki no isu desu.
[Wood of chair is]
The chair is of wood.   It is a wooden chair.

---

* In dependent clauses, *no* is often used to indicate the subject of the clause:

Kore ga kare no tateta tera desu.
[this *sj* he *sj* built temple is]
This is the temple which he built.

The Japanese dependent clause is difficult for an English speaker, and it is discussed in more detail on page 83.   We mention it here only so that you will not be bewildered by this use of *no* if you come upon it.

(3) origin, time, place, apposition.

Koko no wa mina firumu de gozaimasu.
[here of as-for all film being is]
As for what's here, they are all films.   There is nothing
here but film.

to can sometimes be translated "with" (meaning accompaniment) and sometimes "and."

Kondōsan to Chūshingura o mi ni yukimashita.
[Kondō-Mr. with Chūshingura *oj* see to went]
I went with Mr. Kondō to see the Chūshingura play.   Mr.
Kondō and I went to see the Chūshingura.

Satō to shio to kome o katta.
[sugar and salt and rice *oj* bought]
I bought sugar and salt and rice.

to is not always equivalent to the English word "and," however.
to is used only to link series of nouns or pronouns, and cannot be
used to link verbs or clauses.

to does not mean "with" in the sense of using, or by means of;
for this concept, another postposition, usually *de* or *ni*, is used.

ya is usually equivalent to the English "and."   Like *to*, however, it can link only series of nouns or pronouns.

Tadao ya Kiyoshi ya Shigeru ga Kōbe e yukimashita.
[Tadao and Kiyoshi and Shigeru *sj* Kōbe to went]
Tadao and Kiyoshi and Shigeru all went to Kōbe.

There is a subtle difference between *ya* and *to* in such sentences.
ya usually implies "and others"; *to* usually implies "and that is
all."   Thus, the sentence given under *to*:

Satō to shio to kome o katta.

implies "I bought sugar and salt and rice and nothing more."
But the sentence illustrating the use of *ya*, above, implies that
besides Tadao and Kiyoshi and Shigeru there were others who
went.   In English we are usually not aware of this distinction,

but it is well if you recognize its existence in Japanese, even though you may not use it yourself.

kara is similar to the English preposition "from," and indicates either space or time: *made* is similar to "until" or "as far as" or "up to."

> Koko kara Yokohama made dono kurai desu ka?
> [here from, Yokohama up-to, what amount is *qu*]
> How far is it from here to Yokohama?

kore kara	sore kara
[this from]	[that from]
after this, from now on	after that, and then, next
kyō made	osoku made
[today until]	[late until]
until today, up to today	until late

ni can usually be translated as "in" or "to," although it also has many idiomatic uses that may be translated by "at" or "on" or by other English prepositions.

(1) indicating time or location:

> Kisha wa hachi-ji ni demasu.
> [train as-for eight-o'clock at leaves]
> The train leaves at eight.

> Takusan no otera ga Nikko ni arimasu.
> [many of *hon*-temples *sj* Nikko in are]
> There are many temples in Nikko.

> Kare wa doyōbi ni mairimasu.
> [he as-for Saturday on arrive]
> He arrives on Saturday

(2) indicating an indirect object:

> Anata wa Hanako ni tegami o okurimashita ka?
> [you as-for Hanako to letter *oj* sent *qu*]
> Did you send a letter to Hanako?

(3) with verbs meaning "to become" or "to seem":

> Kodomo wa kanai ni nite imasu.
> [child as-for wife to resembling is]
> My child takes after my wife.

> Kisha de byōki ni narimashita.
> [train on sick to became]
> He became sick on the train.

e indicates motion, and is equivalent to English "to" or "into":

Boku wa asu Tōkyō e yukimasu.	Mori e yukimashō.
[I as-for tomorrow Tōkyō to go]	[woods into let's-go]
I shall go to Tōkyō tomorrow.	Let us go into the woods.

de gathers together several concepts that are not associated in English.   It can indicate:

(1) instruments with which things are done; in this sense it is usually translatable as "with" or "by"; this "with" should not be confused with the "with" of accompaniment that is discussed under *to*.

> Empitsu de kakimashita.
> [pencil with wrote]
> I wrote with a pencil.

(2) location, usually translated as "at," with verbs other than those meaning "to be":

> Daigaku de Nihongo o benkyō shimashita.
> [university at Japanese-language *oj* study did]
> I studied Japanese at the university.

(3) Reason or cause, translated as "because of":

> Watakushi wa shiken de isogashii.
> [I as-for examinations because-of busy]
> I am busy because of examinations.   I am busy with exams.

mo when used alone is equivalent to "also" or "too" or "even":

> Watakushi mo yukimasu.
> [I too go]
> I am going too!

mo . . . mo, when used with a positive verb, is equivalent to English "both . . . and"; when used with a negative verb it is equivalent to "neither . . . nor."

> Kanai mo kodomo mo kaerimasu.
> [wife both child and return]
> Both my wife and child will come back.   My wife and child will both come back.

> Kanai mo kodomo mo kaerimasen.
> [wife both child and not-return]
> Neither my wife nor my child will return.

Some of these particles are also used with verbs. In such instances they are equivalent, roughly, to conjunctions in English, and they require a separate discussion (see page 97). The chart on page 105 contains all of the particles and postpositions grouped together.*

---

* You should also be aware that the words *no* and *de* have other common uses besides as postpositions. *no* (in this usage often abbreviated to *n*) also can be used like the English pronoun "one" ("a big one," "a small one"—but not "one can"). It is also used to turn ordinary clauses into noun clauses or to turn verbs and adjectives into noun constructions. We cover this somewhat difficult idea in more detail on page 84.

> Kare no kaeru no wa futsū go-ji goro desu.
> [he *sj* return fact as-for usually five-o'clock around is]
> As for his returning, it is usually around five o'clock.   He usually returns around five o'clock.

> Akai no o kudasai.
> [red one *oj* give]
> Give me a red one.

de is often used as if it were a participle of a verb "to be," and in many such instances the material that it governs can be translated into English as a predicate nominative:

> Boku wa byōki de nete imasu.
> [I as-for sick being in-bed am]
> I am sick and in bed.   Since I am sick, I am in bed.

Words of Demonstration

In Japanese, the demonstrative and interrogative pronouns and adjectives are very closely related in formation to the adverbs that carry similar ideas about place, manner, and sort. All of these words are formed from four basic roots, to which regular endings are added, to form a consistent and logical pattern. We still have remnants of such a pattern in English, where the words where, what, and whither are obviously related to there, that, and thither, but these patterns are developed more widely and more logically in Japanese.

Japanese distinguishes three degrees of distance, just as Spanish and Italian do: (1) near the speaker, corresponding to the English ideas of "here" and "this"; (2) farther removed from the speaker or near the person spoken to, corresponding to "there" and "that"; (3) at a distance from the speaker, not usually differentiated from the second use in English, except by such expressions as "over there," or "that one over there." To these may be added an interrogative mood or a mood of doubt. The basic roots expressing these ideas are:

> ko- [hereness, nearness]
> so- [thereness, not far off, near person addressed]
> a-   [thereness, but at a distance]
> do- [question or doubt]

From these roots are made demonstrative pronouns, demonstrative adjectives, phrases of type, adverbs of manner, adverbs of location, adverbs of motion, indefinite pronouns, negative pronouns, and many other forms.

The following endings are added to these roots:

> -re   [to indicate a thing]
> -no   [to indicate demonstrative adjectives]

29

Root	[here] ko-	[there] so-	[afar] a-	[question] do-
Pronouns, -re	kore this, this one	sore that, that one	are that, that one	dore? which, which one?
Adjectives, -no	kono this	sono that	ano that	dono? which?
Phrase of type -nna	konna this kind of such a	sonna that kind of such a	anna that kind of such a	donna? what kind of?
Mode and manner [vowel lengthening]	kō like this, so in this way	sō like that, so in that way	ā like that, so in that way	dō how? in what way?
Location -ko	koko here	soko there	asoko* there	doko? where?
Motion, direction -chira	kochira here, hither, this	sochira there, thither, that	achira there, thither, that	dochira? where? which way? which one?

* Irregularly formed.

-nna   [to indicate type of thing, "such a, this kind of . . ."]
[lengthening the vowel]   [manner]
-ko   [location]
-chira   [direction, motion towards, or preference]

The table on p. 30 will show how simple this process is.

These words do not change to indicate singular or plural, nor do they have different forms to indicate gender, sex, or the role of the word within the sentence. *kore*, for example, may mean "this," "these," or "them."

When you are referring to persons (except members of your immediate family), it is considered courteous to use combinations of *hito* (meaning man, person) or *kata* (meaning side, with an implication of such respect that a personal pronoun would be improper) with *kono*, *sono*, *ano*, and *dono*.

konohito OR *konokata* instead of *kare*	he
sonohito OR *sonokata* instead of *sore*	that person, he
anohito OR *anokata* instead of *are*	that person at a distance
donohito OR *donokata* instead of *dore*	which one

The forms with *kata* are more courteous than those with *hito*.

Kono kata ga Suzuki-san desu.   Kore ga musume desu.
[this side *sj* Suzuki-Mr. is]   [this *sj* girl is]
This is Mr. Suzuki.   This is my daughter.

sono, although normally translated as "that," is weaker in feeling as a demonstrative than the English word "that," and very often is simply translated best as "the."

The Indefinite, Inclusive, and Negative Word Ranges

The interrogative words which have been listed in the table on page 30 are used to form other ranges of meaning: the ideas of "some," of "every," and of "no" or "none." These formations,

	[interrogative]	[indefinite]	[negative]	[distributive]
Pronouns for persons	dare? donata? who?	dare ka donata ka someone	dare mo* donata mo* no one	dare de mo donata de mo anyone, everyone
Pronouns for things and persons	dore? which?	dore ka something	dore mo* nothing	dore de mo either one
Words of manner	dō how?	dō ka somehow	dō mo* not anyhow, in no way	dō de mo anyhow
Words of place	doko? where?	doko ka somewhere	doko mo* nowhere	doko de mo anywhere, everywhere
Pronouns for things	nani? nan? what?	nani ka something	nani mo* nothing	nan de mo anything, everything
Words for direction, preference	dochira where, which	dochira ka somewhere, one of which	dochira mo* nowhere, neither of which	dochira de mo anywhere, either of which

* These forms take a negative verb.

like those of the demonstrative table, are entirely regular. Particles are added to the interrogative words:

ka	indicates indefiniteness
mo	indicates negation
de mo	indicates inclusiveness

The table on p. 32 will show how these words are formed.

Within this table, the *donata* forms are considered to be more courteous than the *dare* forms; *nan* is more colloquial than *nani*. *dochira* indicates "which" in the choice between two objects, while *dore* indicates "which" in the choice among three or more.

Verbs

Introduction to Japanese Verbs

This section is a brief anticipation of some of the more important features of the Japanese verb that are likely to be strange to you. We urge you to read this section carefully before you move on to the detailed explanation of verb grammar. It will probably help you to understand some of the unfamiliar constructions and features of form and meaning that must necessarily occur in the sentences that have been quoted as examples.

1. Japanese verbs do not have different forms to indicate the number or person or gender of the subject of the sentence. The same forms are used whether the subject is I or you or they or anything else. Thus the verb form *kaimasu* could mean I buy, you (SING.) buy, he buys, she buys, it buys, we buy, you (PL.) buy, or they buy.

2. Verbs are very often used without a pronoun subject, as in the example above. In such cases you recognize the subject by context. Actually, this is not as difficult as it sounds, and you will very seldom be at a loss about the situation which a verb describes. If there is a question of ambiguity, of course, pronouns may be used.

You will probably find the Japanese pronounless verbs easier to understand if you remember that the verb in Japanese conveys many aspects of meaning which we think of as belonging to nouns. A translation of the form *kaimasu*, mentioned above, that would catch the spirit of the Japanese form better than our English counterparts, could be simply "act of buying" or "there is an act of buying" or simply "buying."

Whenever we have given sentences in which the verb is not accompanied by a subject pronoun, we have supplied the English translation with the subject pronoun that a conversational context

34

might require. In most cases, however, other pronouns could fit into a translation equally well. Where we have translated "I," you could read with equal reason "you" or "he" or "they" or another personal pronoun. (See page 115, the section on honorific forms, however, for instances where the verb forms or other words definitely restrict the meaning to one pronoun-idea.)

3. There are only two real tenses in Japanese, a present and a past. Japanese is not so much interested in the subtleties of time as is English or some of the other Indo-European languages. There is no true future tense; the present is used to express definite future ideas:

> Tōkyō e yukimashita. (PAST TENSE)
> [Tōkyō to went]
> I went to Tōkyō.

> Tōkyō e yukimasu. (PRESENT TENSE)
> [Tōkyō to go]
> I go to Tōkyō. I shall go to Tōkyō.

4. Although tenses are few, Japanese is extremely rich in verb forms that indicate moods or aspects of likeness, or belief on the part of the speaker, or appearances. Most of these are beyond the scope of this manual, but there is one such mood that is important and must be learned. This is a form which is called the probable mood. It indicates that action will probably occur, is probably occurring, may occur, etc. We have described it in more detail on page 47. *kaeru deshō*, for example, might be translated "he is probably returning," "he will probably return," "I think he will return," and so on.

5. There are several compound verb forms that are frequently used. There is a progressive aspect which corresponds surprisingly closely to the English form in meaning and formation (see page 46). It is made with a participle and a conjugated form of a verb meaning "to be."

> Nani o shite imasu ka?
> [what *oj* doing is *qu*]
> What is he doing?

6. Each Japanese verb has an entire negative conjugation to balance its possible forms. Unlike English, where you simply add "no" or "not" to most sentences to make a negative, Japanese has completely different verb forms to indicate a negative idea. If you wanted to say, "I bought a book," you would say either:

ABRUPT		POLITE
Hon o katta.	OR	Hon o kaimashita.
[book *oj* bought]		[book *oj* bought]
I bought a book.		I bought a book.

To say, "I did not buy a book," you would have to say:

ABRUPT		POLITE
Hon o kawanakatta.	OR	Hon o kaimasen deshita.
[book *oj* not-bought]		[book *oj* not-buy was]
I did not buy a book.		I did not buy a book.

7. You will observe that two versions of the same idea have been given in the sentence above. Each verb has two sets of forms: (a) its true forms made by conjugating the verb itself (the forms on the left), and (b) courtesy forms that are made by using a stem of the verb, and adding to it various forms of an ending whose stem is -*mas*-. (See page 111 for a complete conjugation.) The feeling of the language, in general, is that the true conjugational forms are too abrupt for polite usage in many places within the sentence, and that the politer forms in -*mas*- must be substituted. (This is not a complete statement of the uses of the polite and abrupt forms, but simply an advance hint. The subject is dealt with in detail in the following pages.)

8. Japanese verbs are highly regular. There are only two really irregular verbs in the language, and these are irregular only in their stems. There are perhaps a half dozen other common verbs that are very slightly irregular in one or two forms. As a result, even though there are more forms per verb than there are in English, and the endings used to make particular forms are longer than English endings, the Japanese verb is really very

simple.   Verbs are so completely regular in the way they make their forms that you will be astonished at the ease with which you will master them.

Verb Conjugations and the Basic Stem

All Japanese verbs (with the exception of two irregular verbs, *suru*, "to do," and *kuru*, "to come") can be classified, according to the way they make their forms, into two major groupings or conjugations. These conjugations are usually called (1) the consonant conjugation (or the *u*-conjugation, or the *u*-dropping conjugation) and (2) the vowel conjugation, (or the *ru*-conjugation, or the *ru*-dropping conjugation). The two conjugations differ only in the way that they form their basic and secondary stems; otherwise, they are identical.

The Consonant or U-dropping Conjugation. Most of the verbs in this conjugation are easy to recognize.   If the end syllables of the dictionary form of a verb are anything at all but *-eru* or *-iru*, the verb is automatically a member of the *u*-dropping conjugation.   The possible endings are:

-bu	-mu	-nu	-ku	-gu	-su	-tsu
-au	-iu	-ou	-aru	-oru	-uru*	

All of these verbs form their basic stem by dropping the final *-u* and making whatever phonetic changes are necessary:†

PRESENT FORM		BASIC STEM
tobu	to fly	tob-
yomu	to read	yom-
shinu	to die	shin-
kaku	to write	kak-
isogu	to hurry	isog-
dasu	to take out, to present	das-
matsu	to wait	mat-

* All Japanese verbs end (in their dictionary or present form) in the letter *-u*.
† See pages 133ff.

PRESENT FORM		BASIC STEM
shimau	to finish	shima-*
kau	to buy	ka-*
iu	to say	i-*
omou	to think	omo-*
aru	to be, to have	ar-
toru	to take	tor-
nuru	to paint	nur-

Observe that the stem of *matsu* is not *mats-*, but *mat-*. This results from a peculiarity of the Japanese phonemic system: the phonetic combination *-tu*, which would be expected for the dictionary form, is not possible in Japanese; its place is taken by the phonetic combination *-tsu*. The table of *kana* in the appendix to this manual lists other combinations of letters which are not possible in Japanese.

If the final syllables of a verb are *-eru* or *-iru*, however, it is not possible to tell from the present form to which conjugation a verb belongs.† A few verbs ending in *-eru* and *-iru* are members of the *u*-dropping conjugation, and form their basic stem (like other members of the conjugation) by dropping the final *-u*:

PRESENT FORM		BASIC STEM
shiru	to know	shir-
hairu	to enter	hair-
kaeru	to return	kaer-

The Vowel or Ru-dropping Conjugation. Most verbs ending in *-eru* or *-iru*, however, are members of the second, or

---

* Strictly speaking these stems end in a *-w-*; for convenient exposition we can ignore this *-w-*.

† For example, the word *kiru* (stress on *KI*), meaning "to cut," belongs to the *u*-dropping conjugation, and its stem is *kir-*. *kiru* (stress on the *RU* meaning "to wear," belongs to the *ru*-dropping conjugation and its stem is *ki-*. This confusion occurs, however, only when the words are spelled in the *romaji*, or Latin, alphabet or in *kana*, the Japanese syllabary. If the character for the word is used, there is, of course, no possibility of confusion.

ru-dropping conjugation.   They form their basic stem by dropping
-*ru* :

PRESENT FORM		BASIC STEM
dekiru	to be able	deki-
iru	to be	i-
hajimeru	to begin	hajime-
kangaeru	to think	kangae-
taberu	to eat	tabe-
ageru	to raise, to give	age-
miru	to see	mi-

In both conjugations the basic stem gives rise to all other verb forms in an entirely regular manner.   For this reason it is very important that you understand how to isolate it.

The Combining Stem and the Polite Forms

The most important secondary stem for the beginner in Japanese is the so-called combining stem (also called the conjunctive stem, indefinite base, main stem, or second base).   It serves as the base (1) for forming the polite forms that end most sentences, (2) for expressing wishes, (3) for making various special constructions, and (in some cases) (4) for creating a verbal noun.   It is indispensable to even the most elementary knowledge of Japanese.

The combining stem is formed from the basic stem by adding -*i*- to the basic stem of *u*-dropping verbs and by adding nothing to the basic stem of *ru*-dropping verbs.

u-dropping verbs

PRESENT FORM		BASIC STEM	COMBINING STEM
iru	to need	ir-	iri-
dasu	to take out	das-	dashi-
motsu	to hold	mot-	mochi-
yomu	to read	yom-	yomi-

ru-dropping verbs

taberu	to eat	tabe-	tabe-
kiru	to wear	ki-	ki-

Observe the phonetic changes in the verbs *dasu* and *motsu*.*

The entire range of polite forms is made from this combining stem. Since it is felt that the true final forms of a verb (see page 111) are too abrupt for use (in most circumstances) at the end of sentence, almost every Japanese sentence that you will hear will probably end in one of these polite forms. They are made by adding the following suffixes to the combining stem of all verbs:

	POSITIVE	NEGATIVE
Present	-masu	-masen
Past	-mashita	-masen deshita
Probable	-mashō	-masen deshō

While there are other polite forms in the -*mas*- group, these are the most common, and the ones that you will find indispensable. with these six forms you should be able to express almost any verb idea that is likely to be necessary, if you avoid complex sentences, relative constructions, and other expressions that are not simple.

Watakushi wa ikimasu.   (iku "to go," combining stem, *iki*-)
[I as-for go]
I shall go.   I go.

Watakushi wa ikimasen.
[I as-for go-not]
I shall not go.   I do not go.

* See pages 133ff.

All verbs are regular in the formation of these polite forms, although the two irregular verbs *suru* (to do) and *kuru* (to come) have irregular combining stems:

PRESENT FORM		COMBINING STEM	POLITE FORM
kuru	to come	ki-	kimasu
suru	to do	shi-	shimasu

Five other verbs are slightly irregular in dropping an -*r*- when they make their combining stems:

PRESENT FORM		COMBINING STEM	POLITE FORM
gozaru	to be	gozai-	gozaimasu
[formal, polite]			
irassharu	to go, to be, to come	irasshai-	irasshaimasu
[very formal, polite]			
kudasaru	to give	kudasai-	kudasaimasu
[polite, formal]			
nasaru	to do	nasai-	nasaimasu
[polite, formal]			
ossharu	to say	osshai-	osshaimasu
[very formal, polite]			

These five verbs are extremely important, and their polite forms are indispensable to ordinary polite discourse. We shall discuss the politeness-function of these five verbs in a later section on special courtesy forms.

> Sensei ga sore o nasaimasu.
> [teacher *sj* that *oj* does]
> The teacher is doing it.

> Anokata wa shichō-san de gozaimasu.
> [that-person as-for mayor — is]
> That person over there is the mayor.

> Yamada-san wa irasshaimasu ka?
> [Yamada-Mr. as-for is *qu*]
> Is Mr. Yamada here?

Koko ni seikyūsho ga gozaimasu.
[here in bill (or check) *sj* is]
Here is a bill (or check).

Sensei ga irasshaimasu.
[teacher *sj* comes]
The teacher comes.　The teacher will come.

The Present

The verb form which is given in the dictionary is called the present or the present final.　It always ends in -*u*.

Basically, its meaning is that of the English present, although it is also used to express future time, since Japanese has no separate future tense.　It does not change to show the person or number of the subject, but remains unaltered.　Thus, *kaeru* (to return) may, according to context, mean: I return, you (SING.) return, he returns, we return, you (PL.) return, they return, I shall return, you (SING.) will return, he will return, we shall return, you (PL.) will return, they will return.

Gakusei wa hon o kau.　　Tomodachi ni tegami o kaku.
[students as-for books *oj* buy]　[friend to letters *oj* write]
The students buy books.　　He writes letters to his friend.

Ashita Ueno no sakura o mi ni yuku.
[tomorrow Ueno of cherryblossom *oj* see in-order-to go]
Tomorrow I shall go to see the cherryblossoms at Ueno.

This form is felt to be somewhat abrupt, though, and in usual polite conversation it will be replaced at sentence ends with the polite forms which have already been covered (see page 40). The above sentences would then read, with no change of meaning beyond increased courtesy:

Gakusei wa hon o kaimasu.
Tomodachi ni tegami o kakimasu.
Ashita Ueno no sakura o mi ni yukimasu.

The present final form is still used, nevertheless, in two other places within the body of the sentence: (1) in dependent clauses, with certain conjunctions (see page 97); and (2) within relative constructions (see page 82 for a discussion of this highly idiomatic construction).

Hima ga *aru* toki, shōsetsu o yomimasu.
[free-time *sj* is when, novels *oj* read]
When I have the time, I read novels.

Boku no Nihon ni *iru* tomodachi wa Kanazawa to *iu* machi ni sunde imasu.
[I of Japan in is friend as-for Kanazawa thus call city in living is]
My friend who is in Japan is living in a city called Kanazawa.

The Past

The past tense (or past final or simple past tense) is used to express events that took place in the past, and is roughly equivalent to the English past (I walked) and present perfect (I have walked).

It is entirely regular in formation, except for the two irregular verbs *kuru* (to come) and *suru* (to do).

To make the past tense of a verb in the vowel (or *ru*-dropping conjugation) you simply add -*ta* to the basic stem:

PRESENT FORM		BASIC STEM	PAST FORM	
miru	to see	mi-	mita	saw
oshieru	to teach	oshie-	oshieta	taught
akeru	to open	ake-	aketa	opened
shimeru	to close	shime-	shimeta	closed

In the consonant conjugation (or *u*-dropping conjugation) however, the situation is not so simple. Sound changes are made in certain syllables, according to the final consonant of the basic stem. These changes are entirely regular, but the rules are complex, and it will be probably easier for you simply to memorize the changes, without bothering with the rules of juncture that produce them.

STEMS ENDING IN	FORM THE PAST BY SUBSTITUTING	PRESENT FORM		PAST FORM	
-ku	-ita	kaku	to write	kaita	wrote
-gu	-ida	isogu	to hurry	isoida	hurried
-tsu	-tta	matsu	to wait	matta	waited
-ru	-tta	toru	to take	totta	took
vowel	-tta	au	to meet	atta	met
plus -u		omou	to think	omotta	thought
		iu	to say	itta	said
-mu	-nda	yomu	to read	yonda	read
-nu	-nda	shinu	to die	shinda	died
-bu	-nda	yobu	to call	yonda	called
-su	-shita	hanasu	to speak	hanashita	spoke

Notice that verbs ending in -tsu, -ru, and vowel + u all form their past in the same way—by changing the final syllable to -tta; and verbs ending in -mu, -nu, -bu all change the final syllable to -nda. As a result verbs like yobu and yomu will both have the same past form, yonda, as will au and aru, atta. You must determine which meaning is intended by context.

The following two forms are irregular:

kuru	to come		kita	came
suru	to do, make		shita	made, did

The past tense is used in the same situations within the sentence as is the present. (1) It may be used at the end of a sentence, but it is felt to be somewhat abrupt, hence its place is taken in ordinary polite conversation by the corresponding polite form, which is made by adding -mashita to the combining stem (see page 40). (2) It is the form usually used within relative clauses (see page 82). (3) It is sometimes used before certain conjunctions, although the polite form ending in -*mashita* may also be used here (see page 97).

Watakushi wa shigoto ga atta no de kaerimashita.
[I as-for job *sj* was because of returned]
I returned because there was a job to do.   I returned because
   I had something to do.

Mado o aketa.
[window *oj* opened]
I opened the window.

The Participle

One of the most useful forms in Japanese is the participle.   As we shall demonstrate in the following sections, it is used to form the progressive tenses (see page 46), polite commands (page 51), perfected action (see page 47), suspending forms of verbs (see pages 80ff), and many idiomatic constructions.

All participles are completely regular: they are formed by changing the -*a* of the past to -*e*:

PRESENT FORM		PAST FORM		PARTICIPLE	
taberu	to eat	tabeta	ate	tabete	eating
kuru	to come	kita	came	kite	coming
suru	to do	shita	did	shite	doing
kaeru	to return	kaetta	returned	kaette	returning
iru	to be	ita	was	ite	being
kaku	to write	kaita	wrote	kaite	writing
yomu	to read	yonda	read	yonde	reading

We have translated these forms as English present participles, but it must be remembered that in Japanese these forms are entirely verbal in meaning.   They cannot be used as nouns, as we sometimes use the present participle, nor can they be used as adjectives. Such sentences as "Eating is the greatest of pleasures" or "Coming events cast their shadows before them" cannot be translated literally into Japanese.

Progressive Tenses

Japanese, like English, has a range of progressive tenses that are indispensable to ordinary conversation. Indicating action that is continued over a period of time, they are formed (very much as in English) by using the participle (see page 45) and an appropriate form of the auxiliary verb *iru* (to be). The forms of *iru* which you will normally encounter in this construction are *iru* (present), *ita* (past), *irō* or *iru darō* (probable), or their more polite counterparts *imasu* (present), *imashita* (past), *imashō* or *iru deshō* (probable).

NORMAL	MORE COURTEOUS
suru to do	
Kare wa nani o shite iru ka?	Kare wa nani o shite imasu ka?
[he as-for what *oj* doing is *qu*]	[he as-for what *oj* doing is *qu*]
What is he doing?	What is he doing?
naosu to mend, repair	
Kare wa kyāburētā o naoshite ita.	Kare wa kyāburētā o naoshite imashita.
[he as-for carburetor *oj* repairing was]	[he as-for carburetor repairing was]
He was repairing the carburetor.	He was repairing the carburetor.
matsu to wait	
Boku no kaeri o matte irō.	Boku no kaeri o matte imashō.
[I of return *oj* waiting may-be]	[I of return *oj* waiting may-be]
They are probably waiting for me.	They are probably waiting for me.

On the whole the Japanese and English uses of progressive tenses correspond, although there are two differences of some importance. (1) Japanese does not use progressive tenses to indicate future time, as we do. We say, "Tomorrow I am

going...." Japanese cannot say this, but must say, "Tomorrow
we go...." (2) Japanese often uses a progressive form where
we would use a simple form. In instances where an action has
lasted from the past into the present, for us the progressive
meaning has just about disappeared, although Japanese still
considers these ideas durational:

> kawaku   to dry (intransitive)
> Sentakumono wa kawaite imasu.
> [laundry as-for drying is]
> The laundry *is* dry.

This idiomatic usage is ordinarily found with intransitive verbs.
You need not use it yourself, since it is difficult to apply correctly,
but you should be able to recognize it if you hear it.

Verbs that mean knowing or thinking are often used in a progressive form, even though we would use a simple tense in
English:

> oboeru   to remember
> Anokata no namae o oboete imasu ka?
> [he of name *oj* remembering are *qu*]
> Do you remember that man's name?

> shiru   to know
> Kotae o shitte imasu ka?
> [answer *oj* knowing is *qu*]
> Do you know the answer?

The Probable Mood

Japanese has a special mood which is used to indicate possibility,
probability, belief, doubt, and similar concepts that exist around
the boundary lines of what has actually taken place. This mood,
which has no exact counterpart in English, is used very frequently
in Japanese, and you must be able to use at least the present
form of it.

Japanese is extremely rich in forms that show the speaker's
relationship to what he is saying—whether he gives it full credence,

whether he is in doubt, and so on—and there are several different ways of forming the probable mood. There are slight shades of meaning between the different forms, though these shades are too subtle for correct usage by English speakers, too difficult to formulate clearly, and in any case beyond the scope of this manual. We shall indicate only basic situations.

Each verb has a true conjugational form for the probable mood. The consonant conjugation (*u*-dropping conjugation) changes the final -*u* of the present form to -*ō*:

PRESENT		PROBABLE	
iku	to go	ikō	I will probably go
nomu	to drink	nomō	I will probably drink

The vowel conjugation (*ru*-dropping conjugation) adds the syllable -*yō* to the basic stem:

PRESENT		BASIC STEM	PROBABLE
kariru	to rent	kari-	kariyō
taberu	to eat	tabe-	tabeyō

The irregular verbs *kuru* (to come) and *suru* (to do) have, respectively, the forms *koyō* and *shiyō*.

You should be aware of two important concepts covered by this form: (1) a probable mood where there is a strong feeling of doubt:

Ame ga furō ga kamaimasen.
[rain *sj* would-fall although, not-matter]
Even if it did rain, it would not matter.

and (2) an indication of determination or exhortation. In this use the probable can be only in the present tense, and must apply to a first-person subject (I or we):

Ikō!   Boku ga ikō.
[would-go]   [I *sj* would-go]
Let us go!   I will go.   (with a strong feeling of determination)

As is the case with many other true conjugational forms of a verb, these probable forms of the verb are abrupt in some situations, and in normal polite discourse their place is taken by forms ending in *-mashō* (which is related to the *-masu* and *-mashita* you have already learned). *-mashō* is added to the combining stem of the verb:

PRESENT		COMBINING STEM	NORMAL POLITE PROBABLE
iku OR yuku	to go	iki- or yuki-	ikimashō or yukimashō
taberu	to eat	tabe-	tabemashō
nomu	to drink	nomi-	nomimashō

Ikimashō!   Ippai nomimashō.
[would-go]   [one-cup would-drink]
Let's go! Let us go!   Let us drink one cup.

The second important form of the probable mood is made by placing the verb form *darō* after the present tense of the verb you wish to use:

PRESENT

yuku   to go   yuku darō   will probably go
kariru   to rent   kariru darō   will probably rent

This form is somewhat abrupt, and in normal polite conversation, its place is taken by the present plus *deshō*:

yuku deshō   would probably go
kariru deshō   would probably rent

This form conveys a stronger idea of probability than the conjugational form *ikō* or its polite equivalent *ikimashō*. In questions it often can be translated with the flavour of "Is it probable that...," "Do you think that...." Since Japanese has no true future forms, and the future is at once indeterminate and probable, the probable forms are often translatable by an English future tense.

Karé wa kuru deshō ka?
[he as-for come probably *qu*]
Do you think he will come?   I wonder if he will come?

Ame ga furu deshō ga kamaimasen.
[rain *sj* fall probably but does-not-matter]
It will probably rain, but it does not matter.   I think it will
    rain, but it does not matter.

This probable form with *darō* or *deshō* can be used in the past
tense and in negative forms:

nomu   to drink

PRESENT

POSITIVE	NEGATIVE
nomu darō	nomanai darō
nomu deshō	nomanai deshō
would probably drink	would probably not drink

PAST

nonda darō	nomanakatta darō
nonda deshō	nomanakatta deshō
probably drank	probably did not drink

As you may have observed, these forms are simply the normal past
forms and the normal negative forms of the verb, to which is
added *darō* or *deshō*.

Do not be too discouraged if you are doubtful when you should
use the *ikō*, *ikimashō* forms and when the *iku darō*, *iku deshō* forms.
It is sufficient if you recognize them as probables.   If you use
them somewhat incorrectly, you will probably still be understood.

Commands

Japanese has true command forms (or imperatives), but they
are felt to be very abrupt, even discourteous.   The chances are
that you will not encounter them.   Instead, you will probably
hear commands and requests expressed in other ways.   Two of
these ways you should learn, since they will be indispensable to
you.

In ordinary polite speech the most common way of expressing a command or request is by means of the word *kudasai* (by derivation, "give" or "grant" or "condescend to"). *kudasai*, which does not change in form, is used as the final verb form, and the word which indicates the desired action is used in the participle form directly before *kudasai*.

> akeru to open   akete opening
>
> Mado o akete kudasai.
> [window *oj* opening please]
> Please open the window.

The word *dōzo*, "please," is very often used as the first word of the sentence to make the request even more polite:

> shimeru to close   shimete closing
>
> Dōzo to o shimete kudasai.
> [please door *oj* closing please]
> Please close the door.

When you request an object, *kudasai* is used with its proper meaning of "give," and takes a normal direct object:

> Ocha o kudasai.
> [tea *oj* give]
> Please give me some tea.

kudasai is the normal way in which you will make a request or utter a command if the feeling of the situation is that of asking a favor. The way to order something to be done is with the form *nasai*, which is less polite than *kudasai*, but nevertheless more polite than true imperatives. *nasai* is used in the same manner grammatically as *kudasai*, but *dōzo* would not be used with it.

> Mado o akete nasai.   To o shimete nasai.
> [window *oj* opening do]   [door *oj* closing do]
> Open the window, please.   Please close the door.

Negative commands and prohibitions are not so easy to form. For *kudasai*, you would use the negative participle form of the verb (explained on page 54) and *kudasai*. This negative form ends in *-naide*:

> kamau   to bother   kamawanaide   not bothering
> Kamawanaide kudasai.
> [not-bothering please]
> Don't bother, please.   Don't trouble yourself.

Negative Verbs

Japanese expresses negative sentences in a different way than English does. Instead of using words like "no" or "not" to change the meaning of the sentence from positive to negative, Japanese has a separate negative conjugation, which parallels all the forms of the ordinary positive conjugation of the verb.

We have already given hints of this situation in the section on polite forms (page 40), where it was stated that *-masu* is a polite termination for a positive verb in the present tense, while *-masen* is its negative counterpart. Besides these polite forms, *-masen* and *-masen deshita*, each verb also has its own proper conjugational forms, which are abrupt in meaning. These true negative forms are built upon a different stem than the polite negatives, and you must be careful not to confuse the two stems.

These true negative forms are extremely important in Japanese, and complex though they may seem, you should be able to understand them. Learn the forms first; we shall discuss their use later.

The abrupt negative conjugation is built upon the basic stem of the verb. Verbs of the consonant (*u*-dropping) conjugation add *-a-* to the basic stem to form a negative stem:

PRESENT		BASIC STEM	NEGATIVE STEM
kaku	to write	kak-	kaka-
hairu	to enter	hair-	haira-
kau	to buy	ka-	kawa-*
iu	to say	i-	iwa-*

* Verbs ending in *-ou, -iu, -au* are considered historically to have a *-w-* phoneme within the vowel combination; this emerges in the negative stem.

Verbs of the vowel (ru-dropping) conjugation use the same form
for basic stem and negative stem:

PRESENT		BASIC STEM	NEGATIVE STEM
ochiru	to fall	ochi-	ochi-
wasureru	to forget	wasure-	wasure-

Negative forms are then made by adding the appropriate form of
the adjective -nai to the negative stem for both conjugations of
verbs.

PRESENT		BASIC STEM	NEGATIVE STEM	NEGATIVE	
kaku	to write	kak-	kaka-	kakanai	I do not write
hairu	to enter	hair-	haira-	hairanai	I do not enter
kau	to buy	ka-	kawa-	kawanai	I do not buy
iu	to say	i-	iwa-	iwanai	I do not say
ochiru	to fall	ochi-	ochi-	ochinai	I do not fall
wasureru	to forget	wasure-	wasure-	wasurenai	I do not forget

Negative forms of the progressive tenses are made by using the
ordinary positive participle, plus negative forms of the verb iru
(or its polite equivalents). iru, as you will observe, takes the same
-nai endings as other verbs. (iru, "to be," ru-dropping conjugation, negative stem i-, combining stem i-):

	kaku	to write	
	ABRUPT	POLITE	
Present	kaite inai	kaite imasen	is not writing
Past	kaite inakatta	kaite imasen deshita	was not writing
Probable	kaite inakarō	kaite imasen deshō	is probably not writing
	(OR kaite inai darō)	(OR kaite inai deshō)	

Negative Forms of the Verb

kiku to hear

FORMS OF *nai*		ABRUPT NEGATIVE	POLITE NEGATIVE	
Present	-nai	kikanai	kikimasen	does not hear
Past	-nakatta	kikanakatta	kikimasen deshita	did not hear
Probable	-nakarō	kikanai darō	kikimasen deshō or kikanai deshō	probably does not hear
*Pres. Cond.	-nakereba	kikanakereba	— —	if I don't hear
*Past Cond.	-nakattara	kikanakattara	— —	if I didn't hear
Participle	-nakute	kikanakute	— —	not hearing
	-naide	kikanaide		

* For recognition only.

All verbs are regular in the negative conjugation with the following exceptions:

suru	to do	shinai, etc.	is not doing
kuru	to come	konai, etc.	is not coming
aru	to be	nai, etc.	is not being

As has been the case with other conjugational verb forms, the true negative forms are felt to be somewhat abrupt, and in polite conversation you should use their polite equivalents at the end of a sentence (see table, p. 54). Observe that the polite forms do *not* use the negative stem, but the combining stem.

Verbs Conjugated with *suru*

Japanese has borrowed an enormous number of words from Chinese, just as English has from French and Latin. These Chinese-Japanese words are usually the words of the Buddhist religion, of literature, of science, of high courtesy, of culture, and of abstract thought, just as Romance words usually express similar ideas in English. Some of these words are indispensable to daily life.

Unlike native Japanese verbs, which we have discussed up to now, these verbs of Chinese origin do not make their own forms; they remain unchanged. Instead, they are conjugated by adding to them appropriate forms of the auxiliary verb *suru*, "to do" or "to make." As you will see, the idea behind this formation is not very different from that of such English expressions as "to make ready," "to do justice to," "to do penance," "to make do," and so on.

You will find thousands of these Chinese verb roots in your dictionary. Sometimes they are presented with the verb *suru* in full: *ai suru* (to love); sometimes they are represented by an abbreviation: *ai s.*

The following forms are typical:

chūi suru   (to pay attention)

	NORMAL OR ABRUPT FORMS	POLITE FORMS
Present	chūi suru	chūi shimasu
Past	chūi shita	chūi shimashita
Probable	chūi suru darō	chūi shimashō OR
		chūi suru deshō
Participle	chūi shite	
Present negative	chūi shinai	chūi shimasen
Past negative	chūi shinakatta	chūi shimasen deshita
Probable negative	chūi shinakarō OR	chūi shimasen deshō OR
	chūi shinai darō	chūi shinai deshō
Neg. participle	chūi shinakute	
	chūi shinaide	
Present progressive	chūi shite iru	chūi shite imasu, etc.
Present progressive negative	chūi shite inai	chūi shite imasen, etc.

All of these tenses and forms are made according to the conjugation of *suru*, which is regular except for its stems.

The Verb "to be"

In English we express quite a few different ideas by means of the single verb "to be." We use to it to mean "is located," "has the characteristic of," "equals," and "is engaged in the activity of." Japanese uses different words to express these different ideas. It is very important that you master them, or your Japanese is likely to be unintelligible.

We shall tabulate these verbs first, then discuss them in some detail:

VERB	MEANING	HOW USED
iru	to be located ———	used with living beings auxiliary to form the progressive

VERB	MEANING	HOW USED
aru	to be located, to exist	used with inanimate objects
	to have	the possessed object (in English) becomes the subject with the postposition *ga*
	to have the characteristic of	used with the postposition *de*
desu OR da (abrupt)	to have the characteristic of, to exist	no postposition used

iru   to be

The primary meaning of the verb *iru* (to be) is "to be located." It is used with living things, whether animals or humans, and if the place is specified, "in" is expressed by the postposition *ni*.

The most important forms are:

iru (present)   inai (negative present)
ita (past)   inakatta (negative past)
iru darō (probable)

Its polite forms are entirely regular:

imasu (present)   imashō OR iru deshō (probable)
imashita (past)   imasen (present negative)

etc. These forms are among the most common Japanese words, and you should know them.

Kyōshitsu ni seito ga sanjūnin imasu.
[classroom in pupils *sj* thirty-men are]
There are thirty pupils in the classroom.

Otōsan wa ima uchi ni imasen.
[*hon*-father as-for now house in is-not]
My father is not at home now.

iru used as an independent verb can only indicate location; it can not indicate quality, or number, or possession, or equality, or anything else.

iru is also used as an auxiliary verb to form the progressive tenses (see page 46). In such cases it is translated exactly like an English progressive.

Kisha ga hashitte iru.   Kare wa nani o shite imasu ka?
[train *sj* running is]   [he as-for what *oj* doing is *qu*]
The train is running.   What is he doing?

aru   to be

If you want to indicate the location of inanimate things, you do not use the verb *iru*. Instead, you use the verb *aru* and its forms:

> aru (present)
> atta (past)
> arō OR aru darō (probable)
> nai (negative present, exceptional in form)
> nakatta (negative past)
> nakarō OR nai darō (negative probable)
> arimasu (present polite)
> arimashita (past polite)

etc. These forms are extremely important and you should know them.

Shinshitsu ni wa mado ga mittsu aru.
[bedroom in as-for windows *sj* three are]
There are three windows in the bedroom.

Anata no gakkō wa doko ni arimasu ka?   Tōkyō ni arimasu.
[you of school as-for where in is *qu*] [Tōkyō in is]
Where is your school?   It is in Tōkyō.

aru is also used to translate ideas which we express in English by "to have." In this construction, the possessed thing is made the subject of the clause, and takes the postposition *ga* (see page 92 for more details).

Okane ga arimasu ka?   Arimasen.
[*hon*-money *sj* is *qu*] [is-not]
Do you have any money?   No, I do not have any.

desu

When you wish to indicate condition, or quality, or number, or characteristics, or identity, you will use the word *desu* and its more polite substitutes. *desu* is not really a verb; it is a combination of a particle and verb forms, but for our purposes it is best treated as if it were a verb. It has the following parts:

	ABRUPT	POLITE
Present	da	desu
Past	datta	deshita
Probable	darō	deshō

When you use *desu*, you do not use the particles *wa* or *ga*, as you might expect. *desu* already has a particle within it, and needs no other:

Kore wa boku no kippu desu.
[this as-for I of ticket is]
This is my ticket.

Watakushitachi wa sannin desu.
[we as-for, three men are]
We are three.   There are three of us.

After adjectives you may use *desu* (and its forms) alone, or you may use the particle *no* (often simply *n*) after the adjective. The *no* or *n* serves to make the previous material of the sentence into a noun clause (see pages 84ff).

Kare no byōki wa omoi no desu.
[he of sickness as-for heavy one is]
His sickness is serious.   He is seriously ill.

Pseudo adjectives (which are best considered nouns of a sort, (see page 70), use *desu* as do other nouns.   No particle is needed.

Kirei desu ne.
[pretty is isn't-it]
It's pretty, isn't it.

desu has no true negative forms, and borrows forms from *aru*: *nai* (present), *nakatta* (past), *nakarō* or *nai darō* (probable). They are usually used with the postpositions *de wa*, colloquially spoken as *ja*.

> Sono firimu wa boku no de wa nai.
> [that film as-for I of — — is-not]
> That is not my film.   That film is not mine.

desu does not make polite forms with *-masu*. Instead, other verbs must be substituted, as you will see in the next section.

Polite Equivalents of *desu*

desu and its forms are indispensable in ordinary speech, but there are occasions when more courteous equivalents are needed.* There are several such polite verbs that you can use, the most useful of which are the *-masu* forms of *aru* and *gozaru*.

The polite range of forms is:

	POSITIVE†	NEGATIVE
Present	de arimasu	de wa arimasen
Past	de arimashita	de wa arimasen deshita
Probable	de arimashō	de wa arimasen deshō
		(OR de wa nai deshō)

More courteous still are the polite forms made with *gozaru*:

	POSITIVE	NEGATIVE
Present	gozaimasu	gozaimasen
Past	gozaimashita	gozaimasen deshita
Probable	gozaimashō	gozaimasen deshō

* This applies only to *desu* as an independent verb. When the forms *deshita* and *deshō* are used, as below, to form negative tenses, they are acceptable under almost all circumstances of courtesy. These two forms in this negative use cannot have their place taken by forms of *aru* or *gozaru*.

† These forms are a little too stiff for normal usage, although guides and attendants may use them to you. We include them only for recognition. Use either *desu* or *gozaimasu* forms.

Nouns and words equivalent to nouns, like pseudo adjectives, usually take the postposition *de* to indicate the positive predicate and *de wa* to indicate the negative predicate:

Ikaga de gozaimasu ka?   Amari genki de wa gozaimasen.
[how — are *qu*]   [too good-spirits — — are-not]
How are you?   Not too well, thank you.

Adjectives, however, take special forms before the verb *gozaru*:*

Yoroshū gozaimasu.   (from *yoroshii*)
[fine is]
You are right.   That is right.
Ohayō gozaimasu.†   (from *hayai*)
[*hon*-early are]
Good morning.   (This is often abbreviated to simply *ohayō*.)
Arigatō gozaimasu.†   (often abbreviated to simply *arigatō*)
[difficult-to-have is]
Thank you.

Passive and Causative Verbs

Japanese has an unusual set of verb forms which you should be able to recognize, even though it is not necessary for you to use them. These are the passive and causative forms, which are made in regular fashion from ordinary, simple verbs.

Japanese has a true passive voice (just as does Latin), which is made by adding *-reru* to the negative stem‡ of consonant stem (*u*-dropping) verbs, and *-rareru* to the negative stem of vowel-stem (*ru*-dropping) verbs.

	PRESENT FORM		NEGATIVE STEM	PASSIVE FORM	
consonant stem:	kiru	to cut	kira-	kirareru	to be cut
vowel stem:	taberu	to eat	tabe-	taberareru	to be eaten

* See page 66 also.
† In these two idioms, *gozaimasu* is the normal courteous form you should use.
‡ See page 52 for a discussion of negative stems.

The entire range of verb forms is then made from these forms, just as with any other vowel-conjugation (*ru*-dropping) verb. You will almost always be able to recognize a passive form by the -*are*- portion, but with the exception of the verb *umareru* (to be born) you need not bother with learning them.

The causative forms convey the idea of "caused someone to . . .." They are formed by adding -*seru* to the negative stem of consonant-stem verbs, and -*saseru* to the negative stem of vowel-stem verbs. The resulting formations are conjugated like ordinary vowel-stem verbs:

> kiraseru   to make (someone) cut
> tabesaseru   to make (someone) eat

These forms, too, are given simply for recognition.

Adjectives

The Nature of the Japanese Adjective

The Japanese adjective is the part of speech that differs most widely from its English counterpart. It has tenses and moods, just like a verb, and is often considered to be a special type of verb. In some areas, indeed, verb forms and adjective forms overlap. All of the negative verb forms, for example, are really adjectives in origin, (see page 53), as is the construction that indicates wishing or wanting to (see page 86).

Japanese adjectives can be divided into two major groups: (1) true adjectives of native Japanese origin, which are like verbs in their forms; (2) pseudo adjectives (also called quasi adjectives, adjectival nouns, and Chinese adjectives), usually of Chinese origin, which are formed quite differently, and are more closely related to nouns.

We shall discuss true adjectives first, and pseudo adjectives later (see page 70). Whenever we use the word "adjective" alone, without any qualifying term, it shall be understood that we are referring to the true, native Japanese adjectives; when we have occasion to refer to the second group of words, we shall speak of them as "pseudo adjectives."

Adjective Forms

Basic Stems

All Japanese adjectives, in their dictionary form, end in one of the following four sounds: -ai, -ii, -oi, -ui. They form their basic stem by dropping the -i:

ADJECTIVE	MEANING	BASIC STEM
akai	red	aka-
atsui	hot	atsu-
samui	cold	samu-

63

ADJECTIVE	MEANING	BASIC STEM
kuroi	black	kuro-
shiroi	white	shiro-
utsukushii	pretty	utsukushi-

This basic stem is used to make all the other forms of the adjective.

We shall not describe all the forms which can be made for each adjective; instead, as we do with verbs, we shall describe only those important forms which you are likely to hear. These forms are the present, the past, the probable, the adverbial, the suspending, the conditional, and the negative.

Present Forms

The present form of an adjective is the form that you will find given in dictionaries:

yoi (OR ii)	good	warui	bad
hayai	fast	osoi	slow
furui	old	wakai	young
atarashii	new	nagai	long

This is the form that is used to modify a noun:

atarashii kutsu	new shoes
ii tenki	good weather
shiroi hana	white flowers

Since adjectives are closely related to verbs in Japanese, each adjective is considered to have a part of the verb "to be" within it, and can be used without any true verb:

Sono kutsu wa atarashii.	Kono niwa wa utsukushii.
[those shoes as-for new]	[this garden as-for beautiful]
Those shoes are new.	This garden is beautiful.

Past Forms

Adjectives form a past tense by adding -*katta* to their basic stem:

PRESENT ADJECTIVE		PAST ADJECTIVE	
takai	high (price or height)	takakatta	was high
yasui	cheap	yasukatta	was cheap

These forms can also be used without forms of a verb:

> Kyonen wa denshachin ga yasukatta.
> [last-year as-for train-fare *sj* was-cheap(er)]
> Last year's train fare was cheaper.

These adjective past forms may also be used to modify nouns:

> Kyonen takakatta denshachin wa . . .
> [last-year was-high train-fare as-for . . .]
> As for last year's train fare, which was expensive, . . .

In such instances, the past tense is usually translated into English as a relative clause (see page 82 for relative clauses).

Probable Mood

The probable tense is formed by adding -*karō* to the basic stem.

PRESENT ADJECTIVE		PROBABLE ADJECTIVE	
samui	cold	samukarō	is probably cold

> Fuyu wa kono heya wa samukarō. .
> [winter as-for this room as-for probably-cold]
> This room is probably cold in the winter.

The probable mood expresses a way of thought that is peculiar to Japanese. It is used to indicate a probability, either in the present or the future, a wonderment or doubt on the part of the speaker, and similar concepts. The sentence above could be translated equally well as: I wonder if this room is cold in the winter, I think this room is cold in the winter, etc. These feelings are closely related to those of the probable forms of the verb (see page 47), although with adjectives there obviously can be no emphatic meanings such as the verb often has.

All of these three forms of the adjective—the present, the past, and the probable—are what are called final forms. They can be used to complete a sentence or a clause.

In actual usage, however, these forms are considered somewhat abrupt if they are used at the end of a sentence, although they are perfectly acceptable as modifiers for nouns or in relative clauses.

It is better to avoid them at the end of a sentence, by making use of one of the following more courteous possible substitutions.

(1) Add *desu*, "to be" (past *deshita*, probable *deshō*) to the present tense of the adjective.

(2) Add *no desu* (past *no deshita*, probable *no deshō*) to the present tense of the adjective. In colloquial speech the *no* is often abbreviated to *n*.

(3) Add *gozaimasu* (past *gozaimashita*, probable *gozaimashō*) to a special form of the adjective.

These forms are arranged in order of their courtesy:

Kono hana shiroi.	[abrupt]
[This flower as-for white]	
This flower is white.	
Kono hana wa shiroi desu.	[normal]
Kono hana wa shiroi no desu.	[normal]
Kono hana wa shirō gozaimasu.	[very courteous]

All of these sentences convey the same thought and differ only in courtesy or formality. The formations are explained in more detail in the section on equivalents to the English verb "to be" (see page 56).

As you have probably noticed, the adjective before *gozaimasu* has a special ending. These special endings are used only with forms of *gozaru*. They are made from the adverbial form of the adjective (see page 67), but their formation is somewhat complex. It is easier to use the following table:

EXAMPLES	ADJECTIVES ENDING IN	CHANGE THE ENDING TO	AND FORM
osoi late	-oi	-ō	osō
hayai fast	-ai	-ō	hayō
atarashii new	-ii	-ū	atarashū
samui cold	-ui	-ū	samū

Sono jidōsha wa atarashū gozaimasu ka?
[that auto as-for new is *qu*]
Is that auto new?

Ohayō gozaimasu.   Kinō wa samū gozaimashita.
[*hon*-early are]   [yesterday as-for cold was]
Good morning.   Yesterday it was cold.

Note, however, that this form is used when only extreme courtesy
is intended. *ohayō gozaimasu*, however, is an idiom, and is normal
usage. You would not say *ohayai desu*.

Adverbial Forms

Adverbs are normally made from adjectives by adding the
suffix -*ku* to the stem, or, to phrase it differently, by changing
the final -*i* of the adjective to -*ku*:

PRESENT ADJECTIVE		STEM	ADVERBIAL FORM	
omoshiroi	interesting	omoshiro-	omoshiroku	interestingly
osoi	late	oso-	osoku	late [adverb]
yoi (OR ii)	good	yo-	yoku	well
hayai	quick, rapid	haya-	hayaku	quickly, rapidly

Omoshiroku kikoemasu.   Yoku dekita.
[interestingly sounds]   [well existed]
It sounds interesting.   Well done!

Japanese is stricter about associating the adverbial form with a
verb than is English, as can be seen from the first sentence:
omoshiroku kikoemasu. We, in English, feel that the state described
in this sentence is really a matter of "being," hence not an adverb;
Japanese feels that since the word is associated with a verb, the
word should be an adverb.

The adverbial form of the adjective, as we shall see later, is also
the base from which the negative adjectival forms are made, and,
with some contraction and assimilation, the base for tenses, moods,
and incomplete forms.

Suspending Form

The suspending form of the adjective is the form that corresponds (in some respects) to the participle of a verb. It is either the same as the adverbial form or is the adverbial form plus -*te*:

PRESENT ADJECTIVE	ADVERBIAL FORM	SUSPENDING FORM
aoi blue, green	aoku	aokute

Sono ringo wa aokute, katai deshō.
[those apples as-for green-being, hard probably-are]
Those apples are green and are probably hard.

These suspending forms cannot be used at the end of a sentence (which calls for a final form). They are only used in incomplete clauses (without conjunctions) within sentences. For more detail on their use, see page 79 where continuative forms of adjectives and verbs are discussed.

You could also use the present tense of the adjective followed by the words *no de* (in this case, an equivalent to a participle of the verb "to be") instead of the suspending form:

Sono ringo ga aoi no de, katai deshō.
[those apples *sj* green being, hard probably-are]

Adjectives and Conditions

The easiest way of expressing a conditional form of an adjective is by using the word *nara* (or *naraba*) (meaning "if") with the present or past of the adjective:

samui nara	if it is cold
atsui nara	if it is hot
samukatta nara	if it was cold

There are also true conditional forms, however, which you should be able to recognize. They are made in much the same way as true verb conditionals: (1) for a present conditional, add -*kereba* to the basic stem; (2) for a past conditional, add -*ra* to the final past.

samukereba	if it is cold
samukattara	if it was cold

Samukereba uwagi o ki nasai.
[if-it-is-cold jacket *oj* wear please]
If it is cold, put on your jacket.

Atsui nara mado o akemashō ka?
[hot if window *oj* probably-open *qu*]
If it is hot, shall I open the window?

Negative Adjectives

Negative adjectives are made in the same way as negative verbs:
by adding the proper form of the word *nai* to a stem, in this case
the adverbial stem:

Pres. Adj.	omoshiroi	amusing, interesting, note-worthy
Adv. Form	omoshiroku	.
Pres. final neg.	omoshiroku nai	is not interesting
Past final neg.	omoshiroku nakatta	was not interesting
Cond. neg.	omoshiroku nakereba	if it is not interesting
	omoshiroku nakattara	if it was not interesting
Susp. neg.	(omoshiroku nakute)	not being interesting
	(omoshiroku naku)	not being interesting
Prob. neg.	omoshiroku nakarō	it probably is not interesting

All of these conjugational forms, however, are abrupt, and more
courteous forms are often substituted for them. These courteous
forms are those of the negative conjugation of the verb, and range
through *desu* and *de aru*, to *gozaru*.

	PRESENT	PAST
Conjugational form:	omoshiroku nai	omoshiroku nakatta
(More courteous)	omoshiroku nai desu	omoshiroku nakatta
(More courteous)	omoshiroku arimasen	omoshiroku arimasen deshita
(Polite)	omoshirō gozaimasen	omoshirō gozaimasen deshita

The following table recapitulates the more important forms of a Japanese adjective:

PRESENT ADJECTIVE	BASIC STEM
oishii (tasty, delicious)	oishi-

	POSITIVE	NEGATIVE
Present final	oishii	oishiku nai
Adverbial	oishiku	oishiku naku
Past final	oishikatta	oishiku nakatta
Conditional	oishikereba	oishiku nakereba
	oishikattara	oishiku nakattara
Suspending	oishiku	oishiku naku
	oishikute	oishiku nakute
Probable	oishikarō	oishiku nakarō
Polite form for combination with *gozaru*	oishū (gozaimasu)	oishū (gozaimasen)

Pseudo Adjectives

In addition to the true Japanese adjectives, which are like verbs in many ways, there are other Japanese forms which convey adjectival meanings (and which we translate as adjectives) even though the English classification does not really apply to them. These forms fall into two groups: (1) nouns and pronouns used in adjectival constructions; (2) pseudo adjectives or noun-like words that are used with special postpositions to convey an adjectival meaning.

Japanese is by no means as rich in adjectives as English, and many ideas which we can express with an adjective must be expressed in Japanese by noun phrases with the postposition *no* corresponding to the English construction "of . . ."

Amerika no shufu [United States of capital] The American capital

Nihon no ocha [Japan of tea] Japanese tea

tetsu no fune   kinu no kimono
[iron of ship]   [silk of clothing]
an iron ship, a ship of iron   silken clothing, clothing of silk

Adjectives for the pronouns are formed in this way, too:

boku no inu   anata no namae
[I of dog]   [you of name]
my dog   your name
                donata no tegami
                [who of letter]
                whose letter

This same construction includes some ideas that we consider adverbial in English:

koko no hon
[here of book]
this book (here)

The pseudo adjectives, most of which are Chinese in origin, are very numerous, and are used in most situations where abstract ideas are concerned, just as in English we use French or Latin forms for learned words. These pseudo adjectives have their own peculiar particles, which in many cases reflect older forms that have disappeared elsewhere. They are basically nouns, however, and in normal sentences require verbs to complete their meaning.

A few of the more common pseudo adjectives are:

kirei   beautiful   rippa   splendid
rikō   intelligent   shizuka   quiet
chōhō   useful   kekkō   splendid, nice, fine

When these pseudo adjectives are used to modify nouns, the particle *na* is added to them:

kirei na onna   rikō na ko
beautiful — woman   intelligent — child

When they are used adverbially, they take the particle *ni*:

Kare wa kirei ni ji o kakimasu.
[he as-for beautiful — characters *oj* writes]
He writes letters [Japanese characters] beautifully.

kyū ni	Kanojo wa kyū ni warai-dashimashita.
suddenly	[she as-for suddenly — laugh-began]
	She suddenly began to laugh.

genki ni	Motto genki ni aruki nasai.
vigorously	[more vigorously — walk please]
	Please walk more rapidly.

Just as the adverbial forms ending in -*ku* (in true adjectives) are used before verbs meaning "to become" or "to seem" or "to appear," the pseudo-adjectival forms with *ni* are used in the same situations:

riko ni mieru
[intelligent — look]
to look intelligent

In most other situations these pseudo adjectives are treated like nouns.

(1) Where a true adjective would require a suspending form (at the end of an incomplete clause, perhaps) pseudo adjectives need a suspending form of one of the verbs meaning "to be " *de* is the form normally used:

shizuka de
[quiet being]
Kono heya wa shizuka de yoi.
[this room as-for quiet being good]
Since this room is quiet, it is good.   This room being quiet, it is good.

(2) The final forms (corresponding to the final forms of a true adjective) are made by adding one of the final forms of a verb meaning "to be":

Kirei da.   (abrupt)
[beautiful is]
It's beautiful.
Kirei desu.   (normal)
Kirei de gozaimasu.   (very polite)

The past, probable, and negative forms can be expressed by changing the verb part.

Kirei deshita.   Kirei de wa nai.
[beautiful was]   [beautiful being as-for not-is]
It was beautiful.   It is not beautiful.

Note that you do not add *no* before *desu*, as you might with a true adjective; nor do you make sound changes before *gozaimasu*. *Kirei* is a noun, actually; it never changes, and does not need a nominalizing particle.

(3) The conditional is made with *nara* or *naraba*.

Kirei nara . . .
[beautiful if]
If it is beautiful . . .

Two true adjectives *okii* (large, big) and *chiisai* (small) are also occasionally pseudo adjectives. When modifying nouns, they can take the ending *na*, although the ordinary ending *-i* is equally common:

okii me   chiisai kuchi
okina me   chiisana kuchi
large eyes   small mouth

Comparison of Adjectives

Comparisons are expressed in a highly idiomatic way in Japanese. Indeed, it is sometimes difficult for an English speaker to recognize that a comparison has been made, unless he has memorized the proper speech pattern.

Strictly speaking, Japanese adjectives and pseudo adjectives do not have special forms for comparative and superlative ideas.   In some cases the words *motto* (more) and *mottomo* (most) or *ichiban* (number one) can be used before an adjective or pseudo adjective, to convey the idea of comparison, but the result may not always be idiomatic. It is better if you memorize a few special patterns that you are likely to meet.

If you wish to say, "A is cheaper than B" you must phrase your sentence in this fashion: "A *wa* B *yori* cheap is."

> Ringo wa ume yori yasui desu.
> [apples as-for, plums than, cheap is]
> Apples are cheaper than plums.

"Which is cheaper, A or B?" you must phrase as "A *to* B *to wa dochira ga* cheap."

> Ringo to momo to wa dochira ga yasui desu ka?
> [apples with peaches with as-for which *sj* cheap is *qu*]
> Which are cheaper, apples or peaches?

"A is cheaper" you should phrase as "A is cheap."

Ringo wa yasui desu.	OR	Ringo wa motto yasui desu.
[apples as-for cheap are]		[apples as-for more cheap are]
Apples are cheaper.		Apples are cheaper.

Superlatives are made in the same fashion; *mottomo* or *ichiban* may be added for clarity:

Ringo wa mottomo yasui desu.	OR	Ringo wa ichiban yasui desu.
[apples as-for most cheap are]		[apples as-for number-1 cheap are]
Apples are the cheapest.		Apples are the cheapest.

Sometimes the phrase *no hō* (—'s direction) is added to the main article being compared:

> Ringo no hō ga, momo yori, yasui desu.
> [apples of direction *sj* peaches than cheap is]
> Apples are cheaper than peaches.

Ringo to ume to wa, dochira no hō ga yasui desu ka?
[apples with plums with as-for which of direction *sj* cheap
  is *qu*]
Which are cheaper, apples or plums?

Ringo no hō ga yasui desu.
[apples of direction cheap is]
Apples are cheaper.

"As . . . as . . . ." is equally idiomatic; it is expressed by setting one
of the two objects apart with the particle *wa*, placing *to onaji hodo*
after the second, and then expressing a normal sentence with the
remaining ideas.

Nashi wa ringo to onaji hodo yasui desu.
[pears as-for apples with same degree cheap is]
Pears are as cheap as apples.

Adverbs

The words which we normally translate into English as adverbs are very often other parts of speech in Japanese, where there are few true adverbs. We have already stated (see page 67) that each adjective has an adverbial form. There are also some nouns that form phrases that are best translated as adverbs.

Many words of time and place are intermediate between nouns and adverbs in their usage:

kyō	today	ashita (OR asu)	tomorrow
kinō	yesterday	koko	here
soko	there	asoko	there in the distance

These words may be used with the particle *wa*, or they may be used with *no* to indicate attribution:

ashita no ryokō
[tomorrow of trip]
the trip tomorrow

koko no tegami
[here of letter]
the letter here

The participles of some verbs have also become frozen into adverbial meanings:

kaette	on the contrary, rather, all the more
aikawarazu	as usual, as before
kesshite	never
mattaku	not at all

Undō ga kaette gai ni natta.
[exercise *sj* on-the-contrary harm to became]
The exercise did more harm than good.

Watakushi wa aikawarazu isogashii.
[I as-for as-usual busy]
I am busy as usual.

Kesshite sonna koto wa shimasen.
[never such things as-for do-not]
I never do such things.   I shall never do such things.

Mattaku shirimasen.
[at-all know-not]
I do not know at all.   I have no idea.

The following true adverbs are also important:

taihen (OR taisō)	very	shika*	only
mada	yet	naze	why
yagate	soon	mō	already
ikaga	how	yukkuri	slowly
sukoshi	a little	bakkari	only
motto	more	takusan	much, many, a lot

Other adverbs are formed from the demonstrative pronouns
(see pages 29ff.):

dō	how?	doko	where
kō	like this	doko ka	somewhere
sō	so, thus	doko mo*	nowhere

These forms are covered in more detail in the section on demonstrating words (see pages 29ff.).

taihen atsui
very hot

Kare wa mada kite imasen.
[he as-for not-yet coming is-not]
He has not come yet.

Yagate haru desu.
[soon spring is]
It will soon be spring.

Ikaga desu ka?
[how is *qu*]
How are you?

Sukoshi kudasai.
[little please-give]
Give me a little, please.

Motto kudasai.
[more please-give]
Please give me some more.

* With a negative verb.

Kore shika motte imasen.
[this only having is-not]
I have only this.

Mō natsu desu.
[already summer is]
It is already summer.

Sukoshi dake kudasai.
[little only please-give]
Please give me just a little.

Dō shimashō ka?
[how shall-do *qu*]
How shall I do it?

Doko ni arimasu ka?
[where in is *qu*]
Where is it?

Naze desu ka?
[why is *qu*]
Why is it so?

Yukkuri hanashite kudasai.
[slowly speaking please]
Please speak slowly.

Takusan kudasai.
[much please-give]
Please give me a lot.

Sō omoimasu.   Sō desu ka?
[so think]   [so is *qu*]
I think so.   Is that so?

Doko-ni-mo yukimasen.
[in-no-where go-not]
I am not going anywhere.

Verb Constructions and Adjective Constructions

Final and Medial Forms of Verbs and Adjectives

Every complete sentence in Japanese must end with a final verb or adjective form. These final forms are:

> present (positive and negative)
> present progressive (positive and negative) for verbs
> past (positive and negative)
> past progressive (positive and negative) for verbs
> probable (positive and negative)
> probable progressive (positive and negative) for verbs
> imperatives

Of these forms above, both the polite forms ending in -*masu* and its developments and the abrupt conjugational forms are considered final.

The following forms are medial, and cannot end a complete sentence:

> the participle
> the conditional (either the true conditional formed from a
>   verb, or the substitutes with *nara* or *to*)
> verb stems when used independently

In adjectives, the adverb forms, the continuative forms, the conditionals, and the coalesced forms used with *gozaru* are medial, and cannot end a complete sentence.

This may seem complex at first, but actually English has much the same situation. An English independent clause cannot stand with a participle alone, nor can a conditional sense or other concessive sense.

Kare wa hon o yonde imasu.
[he as-for book *oj* reading is]
He is reading a book.

yonde imasu is a present progressive tense, and is able to end a sentence.

Sora wa aoku, kumo wa shiroi.
[sky as-for blue, clouds as-for white]
The sky is blue, the clouds are white.

aoku is an adverbial form and could not occur at the end of the sentence; *shiroi* is a present form and could not occur independently within the sentence.

Clauses and Verb Forms

In English we can form sentences out of various combinations of dependent and independent clauses. We can have a dependent clause ("When I opened the door . . .") together with an independent clause ("it was raining outside"). Or we can use two independent clauses: ("I opened the door and it was raining outside."). Japanese, however, can not combine independent clauses in this way; all sentences that are not simple sentences must be built up out of dependent clauses and only one independent clause. The independent clause must come at the end of the sentence.

Mado o aketa toki ame ga futte imashita.
[window *oj* opened when rain *sj* falling was]
When I opened the window, it was raining. I opened the window and it was raining.

Dependent clauses are formed in one of two ways: (1) their verb is a participle, or, in the case of adjectives, the continuative form.

Uchi e kite shokuji o shimasen ka?   (participle, *kite*)
[house to coming meal *oj* do-not *qu*]
Won't you come to my house and have dinner?

Bara wa akaku, yuri wa shiroi.   (continuative form, *akaku*,
                                          from *akai*)
[roses as-for red, lilies as-for white]
Roses are red, but lilies are white.

Several of these participle forms may occur in a series.

Ryōriya ni haitte, kondate o mite, oyakodomburi o chūmon
shimashita.
[restaurant in entering, menu *oj* looking-at, oyakodomburi
oj order did]
I went into a restaurant, looked at the menu, and finally
ordered oyakodomburi (a rice dish containing chicken
and eggs).

Translation of these forms depends upon the context of the
sentence:

Sono eiga wa mijikakute omoshiroi.
[that movie as-for short interesting]
That movie is short but interesting.   Although the movie is
short, it is interesting.

(2) The second way of forming dependent clauses is to use
certain conjunctions, most of which take final forms. We shall
discuss these conjunctions in more detail elsewhere, and shall
merely list them here:

ga	but, and	to*	when, if; that
keredomo	but	aida	at the same time, while
kara	because	no de	since, because
ato†	after	mae*†	before
no ni	even though	tokoro e	at the same time as
nara	if	toki	when, whenever

* Can be used only with present forms of verbs
† Can be used only with verbs.

Two conjunctions, however, take the participle to form dependent clauses:

> kara after (only in this meaning)
> mo even if; neither . . . nor (with negative verb)

> Shokuji o shite kara dekakemasu.
> [dinner *oj* doing after leave]
> After I have had dinner, I shall leave.

> Ame ga futte mo watakushi wa dekakemasu.
> [rain *sj* falling even, I as-for go-out]
> Even if it is raining, I will go out.

There is a third way of forming dependent clauses, using such conjugational forms as the true conditional and similar forms, but for the purposes of this simple discussion, these forms shall be ignored. It is enough if you recognize a true conditional form if you hear it.

Final Forms and Relative Clauses

The Japanese relative clause is a very idiomatic construction. There are no relative pronouns in Japanese, and such words as "who," "that," "in which," "where," and "when," when used in a relative sense, are not translated. Instead, the relative clause is treated as if it were one elaborate adjective, and is placed in front of the word which it modifies. This may seem strange at first, but actually it is not at all illogical: in function a relative clause is very much like an adjective.

Before giving Japanese examples, we shall give a few English paraphrases, so that you will see how the ideas occur:

ENGLISH

> the porter who carried our luggage
> the place where we bought the stamps
> an automobile that is old
> an island with trees that are high
> the book that he wrote

JAPANESE

[the] our-luggage-carried porter
[the] we-the-stamps-bought place
[an] old-automobile
[a] trees-high island
[the] he-wrote book

In relative clauses, polite verb and adjective forms are usually not used. Instead, you usually use the normal conjugational forms of the verb or adjective. This is not felt to be discourteous, since the politeness or courtesy in the final verb of the sentence covers the previous verbs.

Kare no* kaita hon . . .
[he *sj* wrote book]
The book that he wrote . . .

Takai ki no* aru shima . . .
[high trees *sj* are island]
An island on which there are high trees . . .   An island with
    trees that are high . . . etc.

Kesa anata no mita Asahi . . .
[this-morning you *sj* saw Asahi]
The Asahi [newspaper] which you saw this morning . . .

Relative clauses have two peculiarities. (1) The postposition *ga* is not used to indicate the subject. Instead, *no* is used. This is really less significant than it seems, since *ga* and *no* are historically the same particle. (2) The verbs in relative clauses, according to context, can be used to convey active or passive ideas when translated into English.

Boku no kaita tegami . . .
[I *sj* written letter]
The letter which was written by me . . .
The letter which I wrote . . .

---

* *no* is often used instead of *ga* in relative clauses.   See below.

In English we distinguish sharply between the two ideas of active-ness or passiveness.   In Japanese the verb, as we have mentioned earlier, is neutral in most cases, since it partakes of the nature of a noun.

Nominalization and Final Forms

Nominalization is one of the most difficult constructions in Japanese, since to a Western mind it often seems entirely un-expected, arbitrary, and logically inexplicable.   To explain it on the simplest level, it consists of taking a phrase, a clause, or even a sentence, and turning it into a clause modifying a special word called a nominalizer.   The nominalizer and the material that modifies it is then treated like a noun, and may become the subject or object of a further sentence.

Three nominalizers are in general use: *koto*, fact or situation; *mono*, thing, person; *no*, thing or one.   (Do not confuse this *no* with the particle *no*.)   The abrupt forms of the verb and adjective are used before them.

Let us give some examples of this in English words, before quot-ing Japanese examples:

Simple: I walked down the street.
Nominalized: I-walked-down-the-street-situation exists.

> (My walking down the street took place.   It is a fact that I walked down the street.   A situation in which I walked down the street existed.)

Simple: The apples were green.
Nominalized: The-apples-were-green-situation existed.

The use of nominalizers is very complex, and it will be sufficient if you recognize them for what they are when you hear them. You can, however, bear the following points in mind: (1) *no* can often be translated as "one": *Tōkyō kara no wa*, "the one from *Tōkyō*."   (2) *no* or its short form *n* is the normal way of connecting an abrupt adjective form with a verb of being, to make a more courteous form:

Ame ga tsumetai.   Ame ga tsumetai no desu.
[rain *sj* cold]   [rain *sj* cold one is]
The rain is cold.   The rain is cold.

(3) *koto* is normally used in idioms to express ability and the idea of ever-never:

Hashi de taberu koto ga dekimasu ka?
[chopsticks with eat fact *sj* is-able *qu*]
Can you eat with chopsticks?

Sō iu hanashi o kiita koto ga arimasen.
[such speak story *oj* heard fact *sj* is-not]
I have never heard such a story.

Kare to hanasanakatta* koto ga zannen desu.
[him with did-not-speak fact *sj* disappointment is]
The fact that I did not speak to him is regrettable.   I am
   sorry that I did not speak to him.

These two constructions (ability and ever) are explained in more detail on pages 90 and 91, respectively.

It may help you to remember these constructions if you recognize that these nominalizing clauses are closely related to relative clauses, which in turn are related to both adjectives and dependent clauses governed by conjunctions. The basic idea behind them all is that it is possible to isolate great blocks of thought and either set them off as entities, or subordinate them to other thoughts or words. We do this to a certain extent in English, too, though such phenomena as noun clauses are more literary than colloquial: "That the Government is a scoundrel has long been plain to us." In Japanese, on the other hand, such balances and equations and dissociations are the height of being colloquial.

* Past negative of *hanasu*, to speak.

Special Verb Ideas and Idioms

Wishing

Japanese does not express the concept of wishing or wanting to do something in the same way that we do. Instead, it adds a special suffix, the adjectival form *-tai*, to the combining stem of the verb you wish to use. *-tai* is treated just like any other adjective, with the full range of true (somewhat abrupt) forms and polite equivalents (see page 113).

PRESENT			COMBINING STEM	WISH FORM
Consonant conjugation:	kaku	to write	kaki-	kakitai
Vowel conjugation:	taberu	to eat	tabe-	tabetai

To list the major forms of this construction:

	NORMAL (abrupt)	POLITE
Present	kakitai I wish to write.	kakitai no desu (ordinary) kakitō gozaimasu (courteous)
Past	kakitakatta I wished to write.	kakitakatta no desu kakitō gozaimashita
Present negative	kakitaku nai I do not wish to write.	kakitaku arimasen kakitō gozaimasen
Past negative	kakitaku nakatta I did not wish to write.	kakitaku arimasen deshita kakitō gozaimasen deshita

You will discover that there is a good deal of diversity in the particles that are used with these *-tai* forms. The easiest speech pattern for you to follow, however, is to set off the English subject with *wa*, turn the English object into a grammatical subject with *ga*, and think of the *-tai* form as if it were an adjective.

> Boku wa ringo ga kaitai.
> [I as-for apples *sj* buy-want]
> I want to buy some apples.

"If"-Statements

The easiest way to form a conditional clause in Japanese is by using the word *nara* (or *naraba*) as if it were a conjunction meaning "if." It is placed at the end of the if-clause, which is constructed normally, with the verb in a final abrupt form (past or present):

> Kare ga iku nara boku mo ikimasu.
> [he *sj* go if, I also go]
> If he goes, I shall go, too.

> Tsukarete iru nara, oyasumi nasai.
> [tired-being are if, *hon*-rest do]
> If you are tired, take a rest, please.

This construction can be used to express any of the possible "if" constructions that exist in English, including contrary-to-fact statements. Japanese does not have the sharp distinction between ordinary conditions and contrary-to-fact conditions that English has. In contrary-to-fact statements, however, you must be careful to put the verbs in the proper logical time forms, rather than follow English modes.

nara is really a verb form in origin, and a peculiarity of its use is that it contains within it the idea of the verb "to be." It can therefore be used directly after nouns, pronouns, pseudo adjectives, and adjectives, without other verb forms:

Asu wa ii tenki nara . . .   Boku nara . . .
[tomorrow as-for good weather if . . .]   [I if . . .]
If the weather is good tomorrow . . .   If it were I . . .

> Sake wa amari tsuyoi nara . . .
> [sake as-for too strong if . . .]
> If sake is too strong for you . . .

The word *moshi* is often used to strengthen the feeling of the conditional statement; it is placed at the beginning of the clause:

> Moshi kare ga iku nara boku mo ikimasu.
> [if he *sj* go if, I also go]
> If he goes, I shall go, too.

Another easy way of forming a conditional is with the conjunction *to*, which can be translated "if," "in case," or sometimes "when" (when the idea of time is not too strong). *to* is placed at the end of the if-clause, and the present abrupt final forms of the verb (or adjective) are used.

> Kono hon o yomu to . . .
> [this book *oj* read if . . .]
> If you read this book, . . .

The *nara* form is probably the easiest for you to use, but in modern colloquial Japanese the true conditional forms which verbs and adjectives make are more commonly used. You should be able to recognize them, even if you find the *nara* construction easier to use.

The true conditional forms are very regular. The present conditional is formed in *u*-dropping (consonant) verbs by adding *-eba* to the basic stem:

PRESENT		BASIC STEM	PRESENT CONDITIONAL
kiku	to hear	kik-	kikeba

ru-dropping (vowel) verbs add *-reba* to the basic stem:

taberu	to eat	tabe-	tabereba

The forms for *kuru* and *suru* are respectively *kureba* and *sureba*.

Adjectives form their conditional by adding *-kereba* to the stem:

takai	high	taka-	takakereba	if it is high

A past conditional is formed very simply by adding *-ra* to the past form of a verb or adjective:

PRESENT		PAST	PAST CONDITIONAL	
suru	to do	shita	shitara	if I did
taberu	to eat	tabeta	tabetara	if I ate
iu	to say	itta	ittara	if I said
yasui	cheap	yasukatta	yasukattara	if it was cheap

Japanese does not distinguish between ordinary conditions and contrary-to-fact, and does not have special subjunctive forms to conclude a condition. The forms usually follow the natural time sequences, and the conclusion often makes use of the probable mood. This may seem a little difficult at first, but actually it is easier than the Indo-European systems. The following examples will show how conditional sentences are constructed:

Jibiki o tsukaeba wakarimasu.
[dictionary *oj* if-use understand]
If I use a dictionary, I can understand it.

Jibiki o tsukaeba wakaru deshō.
If I used a dictionary, I would probably understand it.

Jibiki o tsukattara wakatta deshō.
If I had used a dictionary, I would have understood it.

Ame ga fureba ikimasen.
[rain *sj* if-fall not-go]
If it rains, I will not go.

Ame ga fureba ikanai deshō.
If it rains, I probably shall not go.

Shujin ga sore o mireba odoroku deshō.
[husband *sj* that *oj* if-see surprised probably-is]
If my husband sees it, he will be surprised.

Shujin ga sore o mitara odoroita deshō.
If my husband saw it, he was probably surprised. Or, If my husband had seen it, he would have been surprised.

Moshi kare ga itara hanasu deshō.
[if he *sj* if-were tell probably-be]
If he were here, I would tell him.

Liking

The ideas of liking and disliking are expressed in Japanese by shifting the thought, as in certain European languages, so that the sentence means, lexically, "such and such is pleasing," "such and such is displeasing."

suki, a noun, means liking, or an object of liking; *kirai*, also a noun, means a dislike, or an object of dislike. Both words are used with *desu* and its tenses, or, more courteous, with (*de*) *gozaimasu* and its tenses. The subject of the English sentence is set off with *wa*, and the object—the thing liked or disliked—is treated as a grammatical subject with *ga*.

Ume ga suki desu. Ume ga suki de gozaimasu. (polite)
[plums *sj* liking is]
I like plums.

Kanai wa ringo ga kirai desu.
[my wife as-for apples *sj* disliking is]
My wife does not like apples.

"Can," "could," "be able"

Japanese has no literal counterpart for such English concepts as "can," "could," "will be able," and so on. There are, instead, several different ways of expressing this idea, the simplest of which is as follows:

(1) Place the basic idea, the process which is to be accomplished, in a normal clause without a polite ending:

Watakushi wa katakana o yomu.
[I as-for katakana *oj* read]
I read katakana.

(2) Place after this the appropriate tense and courtesy form of *koto ga dekiru:*

Watakushi wa katakana o yomu koto ga dekiru.   dekimasu
(more polite)
[I as-for katakana *oj* read fact *sj* can-exist]
I am able to read katakana.   I can read katakana (one version of the Japanese syllabary).

Boku wa kanji o yomu koto ga dekimasen.
[I as-for kanji *oj* read fact *sj* cannot-exist]
I am not able to read kanji (Chinese characters).

The grammatical explanation of this idiom is that the word *koto*, meaning thing or situation, becomes the subject of *dekiru*, and the remaining material forms a relative clause modifying *koto*.
A simple idiom indicates ability to speak a language:

Watakushi wa eigo ga dekimasu.
[I as-for English *sj* am-able]
I can speak English.

Watakushi wa nihongo ga dekimasen.
[I as-for Japanese *sj* not-able]
I am not able to speak Japanese.

"To intend to"

Intention is also expressed in an idiomatic way.

Boku wa Nihon e yuku tsumori desu.
[I as-for Japan to go intention is]
I intend to go to Japan.

tsumori is a noun, and the previous clause, which explains the particular intention can be understood as a relative clause: The intention that I will go to Japan exists.

"Ever" and "never"

The idea of "have you ever," "I have never," etc., is expressed in an idiomatic way by the nominalizing expression *koto ga aru.*

This is used in a construction parallel to "can" and "could" (see page 90) and intention (see page 91). You place the main idea in an ordinary sentence without a polite verb ending:

> Murasaki iro no ushi o mita.
> [purple color of cow *oj* saw]
> I saw a purple cow.

and after this the appropriate forms of *koto ga aru*, according to tense or courtesy.

> Anata wa murasaki iro no ushi o mita koto ga arimasu ka?
> [you as-for purple color of cow *oj* saw fact *sj* exists *qu*]
> Have you ever seen a purple cow?

> Nihon ryōri o tabeta koto ga arimasen.
> [Japanese food *oj* eaten fact *sj* exists-not]
> I have never eaten Japanese food.

These expressions can also be understood as relative clauses: The situation in which I have eaten Japanese food does not exist.

"To have"

Japanese has two equally common ways of expressing the idea of possession: (1) the verb *motsu*, which by derivation means "to hold," and (2) a paraphrase in which you state that something exists.

motsu, "to have" (often with the idea of holding) is normally used in a progressive form:

> Watakushi wa okane o motte imasen.
> [I as-for *hon*-money *oj* having is-not]
> I do not have any money.

Since *motsu* normally means possession in the sense either of holding or actual ownership, it is not used in the many idiomatic ways that the English verb "to have" is. You do not, for example, use *motsu* if you wish to speak of "having time"; instead you use the the other construction, as follows.

The second common way of expressing possession is by using the verb meaning "to be"—*aru*—with the postposition *ga* following the object that you have. Thus, the English subject becomes shifted off by itself with *wa*, and the English object becomes the grammatical subject of the clause: as for me, something is.

> Anata ni wa okane ga arimasu ka?
> [you to as-for *hon*-money *sj* is *qu*]
> Do you have any money?

> Sore o suru hima ga arimasen.
> [that *oj* do time *sj* is-not]
> There is no time to do it.   I have no time to do it.

Purpose

Ideas equivalent to "in order to" are expressed by taking the present final form of a verb (see page 42) and placing the words *tame ni* ("for the purpose of") after it.

> Kare wa gakkō ni iku tame ni hatarakimashita.
> [he as-for school to go purpose to worked]
> He worked in order to go to school.

If the main verb in the sentence has a meaning related to going or coming, this *tame* form is not appropriate.   Instead, you take the combining stem of the first verb and place *ni* after it:

> Eiga o mi ni ikimashita.   (from *miru*, "to see")
> [moving-pictures *oj* see to went]
> We went to see a movie.

> Kare wa sono koto o hanashi ni kimasu.
> [he as-for that thing *oj* talk to comes]
> He will come to talk about it.

Quotations, Direct and Indirect Discourse

In English we make a sharp distinction between a direct quotation of what someone has said or thought, and a summarized report of the words. Grammatically, at least, the sentences "John said, 'I will not go'" and "John said that he would not go" are quite different, even though the ultimate meaning may be the same. Japanese does not make this distinction as sharply as English, but in most cases gives the words in the language of the original speaker, without the shifting moods of the English construction.

This construction is used with verbs of saying, asking, thinking, etc., the most common of which are:

iu	to say	omou	to think
kangaeru	to think	kiku	to ask
kotaeru	to answer		

The original statement is given in the words of the speaker:

> Boku no namae wa Kitagawa desu.
> [I of name as-for Kitagawa is]
> My name is Kitagawa.

The conjunction *to* (meaning in this case "that" or "thus") is placed at the end of this original statement, and the sentence is finished with the verb of saying or thinking.

> Boku no namae wa Kitagawa desu to kare wa iimashita.
> [I of name as-for Kitagawa is thus he as-for said]
> He said, "My name is Kitagawa."   He said that his name was Kitagawa.

Since Japanese has a strong tendency to omit pronouns, you must be careful that you understand the context of the sentence so that its meaning is clear.

An extension of this idiom is very commonly met with in idioms about identity of persons and about hearsay or tradition:

> Yamada-san to iu hito ga kimashita.
> [Yamada-Mr. thus call person *sj* came]
> A person named Yamada came.   Mr. Yamada came.

Kore wa Iyeyasu no tsukatta to iu tsukue desu.
[this as-for Iyeyasu *sj** used thus say desk is]
As for this, it is a desk which Iyeyasu is said to have used.
This desk is said to have been used by Iyeyasu.

You should be able to recognize this idiom when you hear it, for
it is very common in Japanese, and is used in many places where
English usage would find a counterpart unnecessary.

shimau, "to end by"

One of the more common idiomatic Japanese constructions is
based upon the verb *shimau*, which means "to finish," "to end,"
etc.   It conveys ideas which we express in English with the words
"at last," "finally" or "to finish doing something."

When *shimau* is used, the other verb or verbs in the clause are
placed in the participle form (see page 45) and *shimau* is used in
whatever final form suits tense and courtesy.

> yomu   to read   yonde   participle
> Kono shimbun o yonde shimaimashita ka?
> [this newspaper *oj* reading finished *qu*]
> Have you finished reading this newspaper?

> neru   to go to sleep   nete   participle
> Akambō wa nete shimaimashita.
> [baby as-for sleeping finished]
> The baby finally went to sleep.

> Gohan† o tabete shimaimashita.
> [rice *oj* eating finished]
> He finished the meal.

"To try"

An easy way of expressing "to try to" or "to try and" involves
the verb *miru* (to see).   We have a somewhat similar idiom in

---

* *no* indicates the subject of a relative clause.
† *gohan*, literally "rice," is often used to mean a meal, or food, just as in English we
use "bread" with the same figurative meaning.

English: "See if you can . . ."   In this construction the main verb
or verbs are placed into the participle form (see page 45) and the
appropriate final form of *miru* is used.

    torikaeru   to exchange, change   torikaete   participle
        Heya o torikaete mita ga dame deshita.
        [room *oj* changing tried but not-possible was]
        We tried to change our room, but it wasn't possible.

           iku   to go   itte   participle
        Nikkō e itte mimashō.
        [Nikkō to going let-us-try]
        Let us try to reach Nikkō.

        Heya o sagashite mita ga yoi no ga nakatta.
        [room *oj* looking-for tried but good one *sj* was-not]
        I tried to look for a room, but there were no good ones.

Clauses and Conjunctions

In Japanese it is not possible to have two equal clauses connected by "and," as is the case in English. You can not say, for example, "I paid for the hat and left the shop." Japanese would convey such a thought by other possible constructions: "Paying for the hat, I left the shop." "After I paid for the hat, I left the store." These two constructions call for (1) participles, (2) conjunctions.

The use of participles: If you have two clauses (or more) in a sentence, and you do not use conjunctions to join them, the verbs in the earlier clauses are put into the participle form:

Ginza e itte miyagemono o kaimashō.
[Ginza to going souvenirs *oj* let-us-buy]
Let's go to the Ginza and buy some souvenirs.

Annai o yonde setsumei o kikimashita.
[guide *oj* calling explanation *oj* heard]
We called a guide and heard her explanations. Calling a guide, we heard her explanations.

In such constructions the relationship between the clauses must be inferred from context. In translation to English, you will sometimes join the two clauses together with "and"; at other times, you will introduce the first clause by "after," "if," "when," or by other such words.

Japanese also has a rich variety of conjunctions for controlling dependent clauses. In all such cases, the conjunction comes at the end of the dependent clause (or clauses), and the dependent material precedes the main clause of the sentence. Most conjunctions are simply particles or postpositions, like those used with nouns and pronouns, but in a few instances they are nouns or frozen verb forms that have lost their verbal meaning. Most conjunctions are used with a final verb form (present, past,

97

probable, present progressive, past progressive, probable progressive—and their negative forms).   In such clauses the verb
that is governed by the conjunction is often in an abrupt form,
rather than in the more courteous locutions with *-masu*.   This
is not felt to be discourteous, since the main weight of mood and
feeling are brought in by the last verb in the sentence—that of
the main clause—and this verb may be polite.

The following conjunctions are used with final verb forms:

to   usually conveys the ideas of "if," "as," or "when";
it does not convey a strong sense or time or
condition, however, but a very slight difference
in tone between the two clauses.   It can often
be translated as "and."   It can be used only
with a present tense.

Basu ga tomaru to mina isoide norimashita.
[bus *sj* stop when all hurrying got-on]
When the bus stopped, we all got on in a hurry.
The bus stopped and we all got on in a hurry.

Sono michi o yuku to kare ni* atta.
[the road *oj* go when him to met]
As I went along the road, I met him.

Nara ni yuku to otera o miru koto ga dekimasu.
[Nara to go if *hon*-temples *oj* see fact *sj* exists]
If you go to Nara, you can see temples.

is also used to "introduce" statements or thoughts,
with verbs of saying, thinking, remembering,
forgetting, asking, etc.   It is placed at the end
of the statement, and can be translated as
"that."   In this case, other tenses than the
present can precede *to*.

Boku no namae wa Kimura desu to kare wa
kotaemashita.

* *au* normally takes an object with *ni* rather than a direct object with *o*.

[I of name as-for Kimura is thus he as-for answered]
He answered that his name was Kimura. He answered, "My name is Kimura."

kara   means "because." (Do not confuse this with the use described below, with the participle of a verb.)

Kare wa amerika-jin desu kara nihongo o hanashimasen.
[he as-for America-man is because, Japanese *oj* not-speak]
Because he is an American, he does not speak Japanese.

toki   (literally "time"). This means "when" in the sense of "at the time that . . ." or "whenever."

Kaeru toki kare wa sayōnara to iimashita.
[return time he as-for goodbye thus said]
When he left, he said goodbye.

Kaeru toki kare wa itsumo sayōnara to iimasu.
[return time he as-for always goodbye thus says]
When he leaves, he always says goodbye.

Sensō ga hajimatta toki boku wa mittsu deshita.
[war *sj* started time I as-for three (years) was]
At the time the war started, I was three years old.

ga   may be translated as "but," "although," or as "and." It does not imply a very strong antithesis between the two clauses.

Kanojo wa utsukushii ga taikutsu desu.
[she as-for beautiful but boring is]
She is good-looking, but boring.

Nyū Yōku ni ikimashita ga omoshiroi tokoro desu.
[New York to went but interesting place is]
I went to New York and it is an interesting place.

keredomo
(or keredo)   can be translated as "but."   It is stronger than *ga*.

Kono apāto wa benri da keredo takasugiru.
[this apartment as-for convenient is but too-expensive]
This apartment is convenient, but too expensive.

Kimi wa sō iu keredomo boku wa shinjinai.
[you as-for so speak but I as-for do-not-believe]
You say so, but I don't believe it.

no ni   can usually be translated as "although."   It is stronger than *ga*, and usually implies a heavy emotional tone.

Isshōkenmei benkyō shita no ni kare wa "c" o moraimashita.
[diligently study did although — he as-for c *oj* received]
Although he studied hard, he received a "C."

Matte ita no ni kare wa konakatta.*
[waiting was although — he as-for did-not-come]
Although I had been waiting for him, he did not come.

no de   means "since" or "because," but is weaker than *kara*.

Atsui no de oyogi ni yukimashita.
[hot since — swimming to went]
Since it was hot, I went swimming.

* Note that this negative form is built upon the irregular negative stem *ko-* of *kuru*.

nara can best be translated as "if." It can be used not only with verbs and adjectives, but also with nouns and pronouns (see page 87).

Kyōto ni irassharu nara kono densha ni onori nasai.
[Kyōto to go if this train (streetcar) on get-on do]
If you go to Kyōto, take this train.

baai is equivalent to "in case" or "when," in the meaning "if."

Nihongo o narau baai konki ga hitsuyō desu.
[Japanese *oj* learn in-case patience *sj* necessary is]
In case you are studying Japanese, patience is needed. If you are studying Japanese, you have to have patience.

ato is equivalent to "after"; it usually takes the past tense.

Sensō ga owatta ato minna wa shibaraku bonyari shite imashita.
[war *sj* ended after all as-for for-a-long-time dazed doing was]
After the war was over, everyone was dazed for a long time.

When *ato* is used as a postposition with nouns and pronouns, it is used with *no*: *sensō no ato* (after the war).

mae is equivalent to "before"; it normally takes the present tense. When used with nouns or pronouns, as a postposition, it also takes *no*.

Sensō ga hajimaru mae wa subete ga heiwa deshita.

[war *sj* begin before as-for everything *sj* peace
was]
Before the war began, everything was peaceful.

Sensō no mae . . .
[war of before . . .]
Before the war . . .

ue ni   is equivalent to "besides," "in addition to."

Kare wa osoku kuru ue ni nakanaka kaeri-
masen.
[he as-for late come besides — readily not-
return]
Besides coming late, he doesn't return (leave)
very readily.

When used as a postposition with a noun or
pronoun, and the further postposition *no*, *ue ni*
means "on top of," "over," "on":

Tsukue no ue ni . . .
[desk of surface on . . .]
On top of the desk . . .

kawari ni   is equivalent to "instead of."
Eiga e yuku kawari ni uchi de terebi o mimashō.
[movies to go instead of home at TV *oj* let-us-
see]
Instead of going to the movies, let us stay home
and watch TV.

When used as a postposition with nouns or
pronouns, *no* is added:

Eiga no kawari ni . . .
[movies of instead of . . .]
Instead of movies . . .

A few conjunctions do not take the final forms of a verb or adjective, but take the participle; these are:

kara   meaning "after."   Do not confuse this with *kara* meaning "because," which takes a final form.

> Chūshoku o tabete kara dekakemasu.
> [lunch *oj* eating after leave]
> After eating lunch, I shall leave.

mo   strengthens the opposition inherent within the participle, and can best be translated as "even if," "even though." *tatoe* is sometimes placed at the beginning of the clause:

> (Tatoe) ame ga futte *mo* asu dekakemasu.
> [even-if rain *sj* falling even-if tomorrow leave]
> Even if it is raining tomorrow, I will leave.

Used with two participles, . . . *mo* . . . *mo* means "whether . . . or"; when used with negative verbs, it is often best translated into English as "neither . . . nor."

> Futte mo tette mo dekakemasu.
> [falling whether shining whether leave]
> Whether it is raining or shining, I shall leave.   I shall leave rain or shine.

> Kare wa naite mo waratte mo imasen.
> [he as-for crying neither laughing neither is-not]
> He is neither laughing nor crying.

The following two conjunctions take the combining stem of a verb:

nagara   this is equivalent to English "while," and like the English word can mean either (a) "at the time that," or (b) "even though."   It takes a final form when used with an adjective.

Watakushi wa shimbun o yomi* nagara gohan o tabemasu.

[I as-for newspaper *oj* read- while meal *oj* eat]

I eat a meal while reading a newspaper.

Kare wa wakai nagara shiryobukai.

[he as-for young while prudent]

While he is young, he is prudent.   He is prudent even if young.   Young as he is, he is prudent.

ni   is equivalent to "in order to," when used with a verb of going or motion.

Kare wa shoku o sagashi† ni Tōkyō e kimashita.

[he as-for job *oj* looking-for in-order-to Tōkyō to came]

He came to Tōkyō to look for a job.

These are the most important conjunctions, although there are many other words of various sorts (nouns, particles, verb forms, etc.) which act in the same way as English conjunctions.

We have tabulated these conjunctive words (together with the postpositional particles) on the following pages.

---

* From *yomu* (to read).

† From *sagasu* (to look for).

TABLE OF PARTICLES

	With nouns and pronouns	With verbs and adjectives (used as conjunctions)		
		Final forms	Participles	Combining stem
ga	[grammatical subject] sj	[Mild antithesis between clauses; sometimes to be translated as "but," sometimes as "and."]	—	—
wa	[isolates from remainder of sentence; sometimes to be translated as subject of clauses; sometimes by "as for . . ."]	—	—	—

TABLE OF PARTICLES—*continued*

	With nouns and pronouns	With verbs and adjectives (used as conjunctions)		
		Final forms	Participles	Combining stem
no	of [indicating possession, origin, material of which made, part, apposition, etc.] [grammatical subject of dependent clauses]	[Transforms previous material into a noun clause; often ignored in translation]	—	—
o	[grammatical object of verb]			
kara	from; after in certain idioms	because	after	

				in order to
to	with (accompaniment); and (in a limited series)	if, when ("when" in this instance does not indicate time so much as possibility) that (used with verbs of thinking, saying, remembering, etc.)		
ya	and (in an unlimited series)			
ni	to, for (indirect object) in, on (indicating place) by (with passive or causative verbs, to indicate who did the action) [with verbs meaning to become, to meet, to resemble, to seem, to resemble, etc.] to indicate the direct object			

TABLE OF PARTICLES—*continued*

	With nouns and pronouns	With verbs and adjectives (used as conjunctions)		
		Final forms	Participles	Combining stem
e	to, into (motion towards)			
de	with, by means of at [equivalent logically to the participle "being," often not translated]			
ka	either... or [used in series]	[indicates a question]		
mo	even, too both... and [used in series]		even if whether... or	

de wa	[subject of negative verb] — [used with the non-personal pronouns to form the negative range: "no one," "none," etc.] — neither.... nor [used in series with a negative verb]
keredomo OR keredo	but [stronger antithesis than *ga*]
nagara	while ("during the time that"; "even though")
nara	if
no ni	although
no de	since, because
toki	when ("at the time that")

The Language of Courtesy

As we indicated in the first part of these grammatical aids, the degree of politeness or formality which you express in your Japanese is extremely important. We have differentiated four levels of language etiquette: (1) rude, which you should avoid; (2) abrupt-normal, which in some constructions is neutral in tone, and in other grammatical situations is too abrupt to use to a social equal; (3) normal-polite, which you would use on most occasions; (4) very polite, which is somewhat ceremonious, and is best avoided until you are well advanced into Japanese.

The basic ideas behind these levels of language etiquette are these: (1) Vocabulary, grammatical forms, and even constructions which have the same lexical (or observational) meaning can differ quite a bit in their courtesy level. Actually, this concept is present in English, too, where some words are considered all right for colloquial use among friends, but unsuitable for formal writing. (2) When speaking to equals or superiors, you tend to talk-down yourself and your possessions, and to talk-up theirs. For example, when referring to your own wife you use the word *kanai*, which means literally house-person. When speaking of another man's wife, however, you would use the word *okusan*, which means honorable lady. (3) Directness is to be avoided; everything is to be shaded so that it conveys the connotation "if it please you." For this reason, as we shall see, the direct conjugation forms of the verb and adjective are avoided in some situations, and tempering forms are used (see pages 40, 65); direct tenses are avoided, and probability is invoked; elaborate statements of equivalence (like the French "est-ce que, qu'est-ce que c'est") are used instead of direct statements; incomplete sentences are commonly used. Women, generally speaking, are required to use politer levels of language etiquette than are men.

Honorific Verbs and Adjectives

We have already covered the conjugational forms of verbs and adjectives, as well as the polite verb forms in *-masu* (and other forms) that can be substituted for them. We shall simply list these forms in the tables on this page and on page 113.

Table of Abrupt and Polite Verb Forms in Common Use

aruku (to walk)   aruki- (combining stem)   aruka- (negative stem)

	ABRUPT	POLITE
Present	aruku I walk	arukimasu I walk
Negative	arukanai I do not walk	arukimasen I do not walk
Pres. prog.	aruite iru I am walking	aruite imasu I am walking
Negative	aruite inai I am not walking	aruite imasen I am not walking
Past	aruita I walked	arukimashita I walked
Negative	arukanakatta I did not walk	arukimasen deshita I did not walk
Past prog.	aruite ita I was walking	aruite imashita I was walking
Negative	aruite inakatta I was not walking	aruite imasen deshita I was not walking
Probable	arukō or aruku darō let us walk	arukimashō or aruku deshō let us walk
Negative	arukanai darō let us not walk	arukanai deshō let us not walk

	ABRUPT	POLITE

Prob. prog.
 	
Negative
	aruite iru darō
	   is probably walking
	aruite inai darō
	   is probably not
	      walking
		arute iru deshō
		   is probably walking
		aruite inai deshō
		   is probably not
		      walking

Participle
 	
Negative
	aruite
	   walking
	arukanakute or
	   arukanaide
	not walking	

Imperative
(commands)
 	
Negative
	[omitted]	aruite kudasai; aruki
		   nasai
		   please walk
		arukanaide kudasai
		   please do not walk

The abrupt verb forms are used in the following situations, each of which is discussed in detail elsewhere:

(1) At the end of sentences.   This form is somewhat abrupt, and you would be best advised to avoid it.
(2) In clauses, with certain conjunctions.   This is normal use.
(3) In relative clauses.   This is normal use.
(4) As modifying adjectives.   This is really a form of relative clause, and is normal use.

The polite verb forms are used in the following situations:

(1) At the end of sentences.   This is normal use, and is the practice you should follow.
(2) In clauses, with certain conjunctions.   This, too, is normal use, although the abrupt forms may be used here, too.

Table of Abrupt and Polite Adjective Forms in Common Use

	ABRUPT	NORM. POL.	VERY POL.
Present	shiroi is white	shiroi no desu is white	shirō gozai- masu is white
Neg.	shiroku nai is not white	shiroku arimasen is not white	shirō gozai- masen is not white
Past	shirokatta was white	shiroi no deshita was white	shirō gozai- mashita was white
Neg.	shiroku nakatta was not white	shiroku arimasen deshita was not white	shirō gozai- masen deshita was not white
Probable	shiroi darō is probably white	shiroi deshō is probably white	shirō gozai- mashō is probably white
Neg.	shiroku nai darō	shiroku nai deshō	shirō gozai- masen deshō
Adv.	shiroku whitely		
Contin- uative	shirokute or shiroku being white		
Neg.	shiroku nakute not being white		

Observe that the polite forms are not normally used in relative clauses or as adjectives.

With adjectives, the abrupt forms are used as follows:

(1) At the end of sentences.   As with verbs, this is abrupt, and is best avoided.
(2) To modify nouns.   This is normal usage.
(3) Used predicatively, as final words before conjunctions, or in relative clauses. This, too, is normal use. The probables are not used in relative clauses.

The polite adjectival forms are used:

(1) At the end of sentences, predicatively.

They are not used within clauses or sentences.

The notions of giving and receiving are particularly associated with etiquette and respect: you give something down to an inferior, and something up to a superior.   Hence, a superior or equal gives something down to you, while you give things up to him.   This results in the somewhat peculiar situation that the choice of verb of giving tells you who the speaker is.   *sashiageru* is used to indicate services that the first person renders to another; it literally means "to lift up."   *kudasaru* (literal meaning "to hand down") or *itadaku* (literal meaning "to place upon one's head") indicate services that someone else (second or third person) renders to the first person.

> Kono hon o yonde sashiagemashō ka?
> [this book *oj* reading probably-giving *qu*]
> Shall I read this book to you?
>
> Tanabe-san ni hon o kashite itadakimashita.
> [Tanabe-Mr. by book *oj* lending I-received]
> I received a book from Mr. Tanabe as a loan.   Mr. Tanabe lent me a book.

Empitsu o kudasai.
[pencil *oj* please-give]
Please give me the pencil.

The following list includes a few of the more common verbs that are used with honorific intent for most situations; you should recognize them when you hear them.

PLAIN VERB		SPEAKING OF YOURSELF	SPEAKING OF SOMEONE ELSE
yuku OR iku	to go	mairu	irassharu
iu	to say	mōshiageru (LIT. to raise speech)	ossharu
miru	to see	haiken suru	goran nasaru
taberu	to eat	itadaku (LIT. to receive)	meshiagaru (LIT. food rising)
yaru	to give	sashiageru (LIT. lift up)	kudasaru (LIT. to hand down)
iru	to be	iru	irassharu

Another way of expressing a sense of respect or formality is by using the true passive (see page 61) form of the verb, instead of the active form which the sense would seem to demand:*

Taberaremashita ka?   Ikaremasu† ka?
[been-eaten *qu*]   [be-gone *qu*]
Have you eaten?   Are you going?

Incomplete sentences are sometimes used to convey a sense of respect for the person spoken to:

Ii otenki de gozaimasu ga.
[good *hon*-weather *sj* is but]
It is fine weather   [if it please you].

* For recognition only.
† In Japanese intransitive verbs like "die," "go," etc., can be passive in form.

Honorific Nouns and Pronouns

Nouns, too, can be used in an honorific sense.   The prefixes *o* (usually with words of Japanese origin) or *go* (usually with words of Chinese origin) are attached to a noun when you are talking about someone else's possessions, activities, or situations, or wish to preserve a respectful tone.

ii otenki
[good *hon*-weather]
good weather

oyu
[*hon*-warm-water]
warm water

Otegami o mimasen deshita.
[*hon*-letter *oj* not-see was]
I did not see your letter.

You would not speak of your own letter as *otegami*, since the *o* is honorific, but simply as *tegami*.

In some words these honorific prefixes are so standardized that they have lost any honorific meaning, and are best simply thought of as part of the word:

ocha   tea   gohan   rice, food

Honorifics are quite idiomatic in Japanese, for there are some nouns which do not take honorific prefixes.   As a result, you had better not make your own honorifics, but be content to use forms that you have learned or heard in conversation.

If you are referring to someone else's relations, you use a different vocabulary than if you are speaking about your own:

YOUR OWN		SOMEONE ELSE'S	
		POLITE	VERY POLITE
wife	kanai	okusan	okusama
father	chichi	otōsan	otōsama
mother	haha	okāsan	okāsama
son	musuko	musukosan	go shisoku
daughter	musume	musumesan	o jōsama

We have covered pronouns in some detail in the earlier part of the book.   Let us recapitulate by saying that

watakushi	I	watakushitachi OR watakushidomo	we
anata	you	anatatachi OR anatagata	you
kare	he	karera OR anokata	(they, MASC.)
kanojo	she	kanojotachi	(they, FEM.)
anokata	he or she		

are the polite forms that you would normally use, while *boku* (I), *kimi* (you, SING.) *bokutachi* (we), *kimitachi* (you, PL.) are less formal words that you would use to intimates or members of your family.

Word Order

Word order in Japanese is very important, and is relatively rigid, especially when particles are sometimes omitted in rapid colloquial speech and word order is the criterion for determining the meaning of a sentence.

If all the elements of a clause are present, the following is the basic pattern of word order:

> dissociated material (if any)—subject—indirect object—direct object—verb form

If particles are properly given, this word order need not be rigidly observed, except that the verb *always* comes at the end of the clause or sentence.

Expressions of time usually precede expressions of place.　They may both precede the subject, whether they are isolated by the dissociating particle *wa*, or whether they have other particles, or none at all.　They may also be placed immediately before the verb.　Adverbs of manner or degree normally immediately precede the verb.

Adjectives precede the noun they modify.

Particles and conjunctions always follow the material they control.

Relative clauses always precede the word they modify.　Within themselves relative clauses follow the same rules of word order as sentences.

Dependent clauses always come first in a sentence.

The following sentences will show how words and elements are placed in ordinary sentences:

Kesa boku　wa　　kare　　ni　omiyage　o　　ageta.
adv.　subject part. indir.-obj. part. dir.-obj. part.　verb
[this-morning I as-for him to souvenir *oj* gave]
I gave him a souvenir this morning.

Kinō boku ga atarashii uchi ni hikkoshita no de,
adv. subject part. adjective noun part.   verb   conj.

[yesterday I *sj* new $\begin{Bmatrix} \text{place where} \\ \text{house} \quad \text{to} \end{Bmatrix}$ moved since,

kare   wa kyō isoide   yatte   kite,
subject part. adv. verb   verb   verb
                participle participle participle
he as-for today hurrying bringing-coming

boku   ni   kare no kaita e   o kuremashita.
indir. part. subject part. verb noun dir.-   verb
  obj.   relative clause   obj.

I to he *sj* painted picture *oj* gave]
    Because I moved into a new home yesterday, he came in a hurry
today, and gave me a picture which he had painted.

    The first material within large brackets is a dependent clause,
ending in *no de*; the phrase *kare no kaita* is a relative clause.

Forming Questions

Most Japanese complete sentences can be turned into questions by adding at their very end the particle *ka*, which is the equivalent of a question mark.

POSITIVE	INTERROGATIVE
Kore wa anata no desu.	Kore wa anata no desu ka?
[this as-for you of is]	Is this yours?
This is yours.	

The particle *ne*, which is also placed at the end of a sentence is the equivalent of "n'est-ce pas" or "nicht wahr," and can be translated as "isn't it," or "don't you think," or something similar.

Ii tenki desu ne.
[good weather is not-so]
It's fine weather, isn't it?

Questions that occur in the probable mood (see page 47) often do not require the particle *ka* in order to be questions although in this situation an affirmative answer is usually anticipated. Rising tone at the end of the sentence indicates a question.

Ashita iku deshō?
[tomorrow go probably]
We shall probably go tomorrow?

Questions are also made with interrogative pronouns and certain adverbs or conjunctions:

itsu desu ka?	when is it?
doko desu ka?	where is it?
nan desu ka?	what is it?

$\left.\begin{cases} \text{dochira* desu ka?} \\ \text{doret desu ka?} \end{cases}\right\}$ which one is it?

dare desu ka?   who is it?

nanji desu ka?   what time is it?

In most cases such questions use the particle *ka* at their end.

* Which of two.
† Which of more than two.

Numbers and Counting Objects

The Japanese numerical system is extremely complex, and it cannot be encompassed within this brief introduction to Japanese grammar.   The most that this manual can do is survey briefly a few of the more important features in the use of numbers, so that you will understand the principles behind such numbers as you are likely to hear.   In all probability you will not be able to use the numerical system correctly without further study in a more advanced grammar, but if you follow the hints given in this book you will at least be understood.

Japanese has two systems of numbers, one of which is native, and the other of which is Chinese in origin:

	JAPANESE		CHINESE
	INDEPENDENT FORM	JOINING FORM	
1	hitotsu	hito-	ichi
2	futatsu	futa-	ni
3	mittsu	mi-	san
4	yottsu	yo-	shi
5	itsutsu	itsu-	go
6	muttsu	mu-	roku
7	nanatsu	nana-	shichi
8	yattsu	ya-	hachi
9	kokonotsu	kokono-	ku (or kyū)
10	to	to-	jū

After 10, only Chinese numerals are used.   Their forms are regular, except for occasional phonetic changes that are optional.

11	jū ichi	13	jū san
12	jū ni	14	jū shi

15	jū go	30	san jū
16	jū roku	40	shi jū OR yon jū
17	jū shichi	100	hyaku
18	jū hachi	108	hyaku hachi
19	jū ku	200	ni hyaku
20	ni jū	1000	issen OR sen
21	ni jū ichi	10,000	ichi man

Although the true Chinese number for four is *shi*, the Japanese number, *yon*, is often substituted for *shi* (in some combinations) since *shi* is also the Japanese root meaning death, and its use was considered inauspicious.

Use of these two sets of numbers is complex and highly idiomatic, as you will see in later sections of this chapter. At this point we shall indicate only a few of the situations in which each type of numeral is used.

The Japanese forms are used

(a) In statements of age:

Hanako no toshi wa ikutsu desu ka?   Muttsu desu.
[Hanako of years as-for how-many is *qu*.   Six is.]
How old is Hanako?   She is six.   (She is six years old.)

(b) When mentioning quantities of objects (not persons):

Mittsu kudasai.   Futatsu dake arimasen.
[Three please-give.   Two only are-not]
Please give me three.   There are only two.

We shall describe this use of Japanese numerals in more detail in the section describing classifiers, at which point it will be seen that the situation on this usage is very complex.

The Chinese forms are used when talking about measures of time, distance, and money, with the following words:

ji	o'clock	*nen*	year
en	yen	*sen*	"cent"
fun	minute	*kai*	story of a building
shaku	foot		

Kakitomeryō o awasete jū en desu.
[Registration-fee *oj* including ten yen is]
Including the registration fee, it is ten yen.

fun and *sen* undergo phonetic changes when they are combined with numerals. These changes are indicated in the table of classifiers and numerals on page 125.

Classifiers

One of the most difficult features of the numerical system is the concept of classifiers, or special words that are used with numbers to show the categories of different things. In English we speak of three head of cattle, two hands of cards, two sheets of paper, five pieces of cake, and so on. Japanese has carried this idea much farther, so that most articles must be described in terms of words like head, hand, sheet, and so on. Thus, one speaks of five persons of carpenters, two cylinders of pencils, two surfaces of paper, coins, or coats, and so on.

There are many of these classifiers in use in Japanese, but we shall list only the most common:

nin	used with human beings
hiki	used with animals
hon	with long, slender objects like sticks, pencils, arms, etc.
satsu	with books or magazines
mai	with flat things like paper, coins, clothing
hai	cups full, pots full, etc.
chaku	suits of clothing
soku	pairs of shoes and stockings
kire	slice of meat, fish, cake, etc.
ko	item, used generally

Some of these classifiers are used with the Chinese numbers, while others are used with the Japanese combining forms. Phonetic changes are frequent with these forms, as you can see from the table which follows:

	1	2	3	4	5	6	7	8	9	10	how many
nin, used with humans	hitori	futari	sannin	yonin	gonin	rokunin	shichinin	hachinin	kunin	jūnin	nannin
hiki, used with animals	ippiki	nihiki	sambiki	yonhiki	gohiki	roppiki	shichihiki or nanahiki	hachihiki	kyūhiki	jippiki	nambiki
hon, used with long slender objects	ippon	nihon	sambon	shihon	gohon	roppon	shichihon or nanahon	hachihon or happon	kyūhon	jippon	nambon
satsu, used with books, magazines, etc.	issatsu	nisatsu	sansatsu	shisatsu	gosatsu	rokusatsu	shichisatsu or nanasatsu	hassatsu	kyūsatsu	jissatsu	nansatsu
mai, with flat sheetlike objects	ichimai	nimai	sammai	yomai or yonmai	gomai	rokumai	nanamai	hachimai	kyūmai	jūmai	nammai
hai, cups full etc.	ippai	nihai	sambai	yonhai	gohai	rokuhai or roppai	nanahai	hachihai or happai	kyūhai	jippai	nambai
chaku, suits of clothing	itchaku	nichaku	sanchaku	yonchaku	gochaku	rokuchaku	nanachaku	hatchaku	kyū-chaku	jitchaku	nanchaku
soku, pairs of shoes, etc	issoku	nisoku	sanzoku	yonsoko	gosoku	rokusoku	nanasoku	hassoku	kyūsoku	jissoku	nanzoku
kire, slice of	hitokire	futakire	mikire	yokire	itsukire	mukire	nanakire	yakire	kyūkire	tokire	ikukire
ko, table, used with almost anything	ikko	niko	sanko	yonko	goko	rokko	nanako	hakko	kyūko	jikko	nanko
fun, minute	ippun	nifun	sampun	yonfun	gofun	roppun	shichifun or nanafun	hachifun	kyūfun	jippun	nanpun
sen, "cent"	issen	nisen	sansen	yonsen	gosen	rokusen	shichisen or nansen	hassen	kyūsen	jissen	nansen

Where a definite classifier is not called for, Japanese usually applies the independent forms of the Japanese range of numbers: *hitotsu, futatsu, mittsu,* etc. If you wish, you can use this group as numbers whenever you talk about things or objects (though not about human beings). This may not always be correct, but it will always be intelligible.

Numbers are used grammatically in three ways: (1) alone, (2) after the noun, or (3) with *no* before the noun.

(1)   sambon
      three

(2)   empitsu sambon
      [pencils three-cylinders]
      three pencils

(3)   sambon no empitsu
      [3-cylinders of pencils]
      three pencils

Ringo ga mittsu aru.
[apples *sj* three are]
There are three apples.

Mittsu no ringo ga aru.
[three of apples *sj* are]
There are three apples.

Ringo o mittsu kudasai.
[apples *oj* three give]
Please give me three apples.

Kōhii ippai ikaga desu ka?
[coffee one-cup how is *qu*]
How about a cup of coffee?

Ippai kudasai.
[one-cup give]
Please give me a cup (of coffee).

Dates and Telling Time

Two systems of giving the year are used in Japan.   The Japanese way is to speak of the —th year of whatever Emperor is reigning. Thus, 1962 would be Shōwa (the era of the Emperor Hirohito) thirty-seven:

Shōwa san jū shichi nen
[Shōwa three ten seven year]
the 37th year of Shōwa

One can also use the Christian system:

sen kyūhyaku roku jū ni nen
[thousand nine-hundred six ten two year]
1962

The months are formed by the Chinese numerals and the word
gatsu, meaning month, in combinations:

ichigatsu   January
nigatsu   February
sangatsu   March
shigatsu   April
etc.

The days of the month are slightly irregular in formation:

1st	tsuitachi	11th	jūichinichi	21st	nijūichinichi
2nd	futsuka	12th	jūninichi	22nd	nijūninichi
3rd	mikka	13th	jūsannichi	23rd	nijūsannichi
4th	yokka	14th	jūyokka	24th	nijuyokka
5th	itsuka	15th	jūgonichi	25th	nijūgonichi
6th	muika	16th	jūrokunichi	26th	nijūrokunichi
7th	nanoka	17th	jūshichinichi	27th	nijūshichinichi
8th	yōka	18th	jūhachinichi	28th	nijūhachinichi
9th	kokonoka	19th	jūkunichi	29th	nijūkunichi
10th	tōka	20th	hatsuka	30th	sanjūnichi
				31st	sanjūichinichi

Kyō wa nannichi desu ka?
[today as-for what-day is *qu*]
What day is today?

Kyō wa sen kyūhyaku roku jū nen hachigatsu jūrokunichi
desu.
[today as-for 1000 900 6 10 year August 16th is]
Today is August 16th, 1960.

The hours are formed by using the Chinese numerals and the word *ji*:

ichiji	one	goji	five	kuji	nine
niji	two	rokuji	six	jūji	ten
sanji	three	shichiji	seven	jūichiji	eleven
yoji	four	hachiji	eight	jūniji	twelve

A.M. is expressed by placing *gozen* before the number of the hour; P.M., by placing *gogo* before the hour. Noon is *hiru*. Midnight is *mayonaka*.

The minutes are expressed by a combination of the Chinese numerals and the word *fun*; phonetic combinations occur in several numbers.

1 minute	ippun	13 minutes	jūsampun
2 minutes	nifun	14 minutes	jūyompun
3 minutes	sampun	15 minutes	jūgofun
4 minutes	yompun	16 minutes	jūroppun
5 minutes	gofun	17 minutes	jūshichifun
6 minutes	roppun	18 minutes	jūhachifun
7 minutes	shichifun		(OR jūhappun)
	(OR nanafun)	19 minutes	jūkyūfun
8 minutes	hachifun	20 minutes	nijippun
	(OR happun)	21 minutes	nijūippun
9 minutes	kyūfun	30 minutes	sanjippun (OR han
10 minutes	jippun		(meaning "half"))
11 minutes	jūichifun	31 minutes	sanjūippun
	(OR jūippun)	40 minutes	yonjippun
12 minutes	jūnifun	50 minutes	gojippun

The intermediate numbers are formed regularly in the same manner as the 20 minute series.

To express minutes after, you use the word *sugi* after the number of minutes; to express minutes before, you use the word *mae* after the number of minutes.

Nanji desu ka?	Shichiji desu.
[what time is *qu*]	[seven-o'clock is]
What time is it?	It is seven.

Gogo shichiji gofun mae (sugi) desu.
[P.M. seven-o'clock five-minutes before (after) is]
It is five minutes before (after) seven P.M.   It is 6:55 (7:05)
P.M.

Gozen shichiji han desu.
[A.M. seven-o'clock half is]
It is half past seven A.M.

Idiomatic Expressions

Japanese is rich in idiomatic expressions of courtesy, most of which do not lend themselves easily to grammatical analysis. It would be impossible to list more than a few of them. Others can be found in a good phrase book or a more extensive grammar.

okinodoku desu	I am very sorry [to hear it].
goran nasai	Look!
arigatō [gozaimashita]	Thank you.
omachidō sama	I'm sorry to have kept you waiting.
okagesama de	Thanks to you. (usually untranslated)
ojama itashimashita	Sorry to have bothered you. (when leaving someone's house)
ohayō gozaimasu	Good morning.
oyasumi nasai	Good night.
komban wa	Good evening.
konnichi wa	Good day. Good morning. Hello.
sayōnara	Au revoir. Goodbye.
gomen nasai	Excuse me. I am sorry. Pardon me.
sumimasen	Excuse me. I am sorry. Pardon me.
shitsurei itashimasu	Excuse me—I must leave. May I come in?
chotto haiken	May I look at it?
dō itashimashite	You're welcome. Not at all.
hajimemashite	Pleased to meet you.
dōzo yoroshiku	Pleased to meet you.
shikata ga nai	I'm sorry, but there's nothing one can do about it. What can you do about it?
omedetō gozaimasu	congratulations.
dōmo	[usually understood from context as part of a sentence: Thank you, not at all, I'm sorry, I'm embarrassed, etc.].

Appendix: Japanese Pronunciation

Japanese is relatively easy for an English-speaker to pronounce, since there are very few sounds that do not appear in English, and Japanese sound combinations are simple. The following table will summarize the most important features:

a   as in f*a*ther

ā   as in f*a*ther, but held longer

b   as in *b*at

ch   as in *ch*at

d   as in *d*ental

e   as in m*e*n

ē   as in m*e*n, but held longer

f   unlike English *f*. Formed by bringing the lower lip up so that it almost touches the upper lip, then holding the position and trying to say an *f*. (English *f*, on the other hand, is formed by bringing the lower lip up to touch the teeth.) If you cannot manage the Japanese f, the English *f* will always be intelligible.

g   as in *g*o. In the middle of words and in the particle *ga* in standard Japanese, g is often pronounced like *ng* in so*ng*. But an English *g* is always intelligible and correct.

h   as in *h*ome. In the syllable *hi*, however, h is pronounced like a harsh *sh* or *ch* in German i*ch*.

i   as in benz*i*ne.

ii   as in benz*i*ne, but held longer

j   as in *j*et

k   as in *c*at

m   as in *m*at

n   as in *n*et. At the end of words n is often pronounced by Tōkyō speakers as if it were halfway between *n* and *ng* (in si*ng*).   An ordinary *n* is always intelligible, and is not incorrect.

o   as in *n*otify.   Pronounce this as a single pure sound, not as a diphthong; English *o* is a diphthong of *o–u*.

ō   as in *n*otify, but held longer

p   as in *sp*ry.   Do not make an *h* sound after the sound *p*, as we do in English in words like *p*in or *p*et.

r   unlike English *r*.   Made with a single flip of the tip of the tongue against the ridge behind your upper front teeth. It often sounds like a *d* to an English ear.

s   as in *s*ay

sh   as in *sh*e

t   as in *st*op.   Do not make an *h* sound after the sound *t*, as we do in English in words like *t*in or *t*en.

u   as in f*oo*d.   Do not round the corners of your mouth when you make this sound; draw them back.

ū   as in f*oo*d, but held longer

w   as in *w*ash

y   as in *y*ard.   y is a consonant, not a vowel.

z   as in *z*one.   The combination *zu* is pronounced *dzu*.

There are certain special situations and general points which deserve special mention.   (1) The long vowels ā, ē, ii, ō, ū are considered different letters from the short vowels, and must be given their full value.   An incorrect long or short vowel will change the meaning of a word: *toru* means to take; *tōru*, to pass.

(2) In some situations the letters i and u are not fully sounded. This usually occurs between voiceless consonants (p, ch, ts, s, k, sh) or after a voiceless consonant at the end of a phrase.   In such instances they are whispered, or not pronounced at all.   To give a few common examples: -*masu* is pronounced *mas*; -*mashita* is pronounced *mashta*; *desu* is pronounced *des*; *deshita* is pronounced *deshta*; *watakushi* is pronounced *watakshi*.   Imitate your record set or speaker on individual words and situations here, since this is subject to many variations and exceptions.

(3) Observe double consonants very closely in Japanese; they

are not simply curiosities of spelling, as they often are in English, but are meaningful. You will change the meaning of a word by making an error in this respect: *kite*, for example, means coming; *kitte* means postage stamp.

(4) Do not stress certain syllables and swallow others; Japanese does not have a strong stress system like English. Instead, pronounce each sound clearly and distinctly, with a moderate, even stress. Pitch of the voice, though it does enter into Japanese, is best ignored by a beginner, since it is difficult to master, and is probably not clearly indicated in the dictionaries available to you. In most situations it is not important.

Possible Combinations and Sound Shifts

The table on page 134 indicates the range of permitted primary vowel and consonant combinations. As you will note there are five basic vowels—a, i, u, e, o—and fourteen consonants—k, s, t, n, h, m, y, r, w, g, z, d, b, p.

The following combinations are not permitted in Japanese: *si* (instead, use *shi*); *ti* (instead, use *chi*); *tu* (instead, use *tsu*); *hu* (instead, use *fu*); *yi, ye, wi, wu, we* (for which the ordinary vowels are used); *wo* (which has a special symbol but is pronounced *o*); *zi* (instead, use *ji*); *di* (instead, use *ji*); *du* (instead, use *zu*).

This table is not as difficult as it may seem at first glance, since it is nothing but the Japanese syllabary in transcription. You will find it useful in two areas. (1) Japanese, like English, borrows words from foreign languages very easily. Therefore, if you are at a loss for the name of a Western article in Japanese, there is a good chance that you will be understood if you simply say the the English word slowly, ending each syllable with a vowel, making the foreign word fit the phonetic pattern of Japanese. Examples: lemonade, *remonēdo*; cheese, *chiizu*; vanilla, *banira*; coffee, *kōhii*; fuse, *hyūzu*; valve, *barubu*; etc. As you will observe, Japanese has no l-sound, and uses r in its place; consonant clusters are avoided by inserting neutral vowels; all syllables end with a vowel or -n. (2) In verb or adjective conjugation, the stem of the

	-a	-i	-u	-e	-o
[no consonant]	a	i	u	e	o
k-	ka	ki	ku	ke	ko
s-	sa	shi	su	se	so
t-	ta	chi	tsu	te	to
n-	na	ni	nu	ne	no
h-	ha	hi	fu	he	ho
m-	ma	mi	mu	me	mo
y-	ya	(i)	yu	(e)	yo
r-	ra	ri	ru	re	ro
w-	wa	(i)	(u)	(e)	o
g-	ga	gi	gu	ge	go
z-	za	ji	zu	ze	zo
d-	da	ji	zu	de	do
b-	ba	bi	bu	be	bo
p-	pa	pi	pu	pe	po

word may end in a consonant in which there is a phonetic change. For example, in the verb *matsu*, to wait, the stem is *mat-*. The present form ends in *-u*, producing *matsu*, since **matu* is impossible. The joining stem ends in *-i*, producing *machi*, since **mati* is impossible. The negative stem ends in *-a*, producing *mata*, which is possible. Similarly, for *dasu*, to take, the joining stem would end in *-i*, and would become *dashi-*.* The past of *-masu* becomes *-mashita*, since the past is formed by adding *-ita* to the stem *-mas-*.

---

* An earlier form of Romanization, which you may meet occasionally, did not follow the phonetic pronunciation, but adhered to the phonemic structure of the language; from this point of view the ts of tsu and the ch of chi are simply positional variants of t. This system would write matu-, mati-, and dasi-. Thus, the name of the famous Japanese vessel was spelled as Titibu Maru, even though it was pronounced as Chichibu Maru.

A Glossary of Grammatical Terms

This section is intended to refresh your memory of English grammatical terms or to clear up difficulties you may have had in understanding them. Before you work through the Japanese grammar, you should have a reasonably clear idea what the parts of speech and parts of a sentence are. This is not for reasons of pedantry, but simply because it is easier to talk about grammar if we agree upon terms. Grammatical terminology is as necessary to the study of grammar as the names of automobile parts are to garagemen.

This list is not exhaustive, and the definitions do not pretend to be complete, or to settle points of interpretation that grammarians have been disputing for the past several hundred years. It is a working analysis rather than a scholarly investigation. The definitions given, however, represent most typical American usage, and should serve for basic use.

The Parts of Speech

English words can be divided into eight important groups: nouns, adjectives, articles, verbs, adverbs, pronouns, prepositions, and conjunctions. The boundaries between one group of words and another are sometimes vague and ill-felt in English, but a good dictionary, like the *Webster Collegiate*, can help you make decisions in questionable cases. Always bear in mind, however, that the way a word is used in a sentence may be just as important as the nature of the word itself in deciding what part of speech the word is.

Nouns. *Nouns* are the *words* for *things* of all *sorts*, whether these *things* are real *objects* that you can see, or *ideas*, or *places*, or *qualities*, or *groups*, or more abstract *things*. *Examples* of *words* that are

136

nouns are *cat, vase, door, shrub, wheat, university, mercy, intelligence, ocean, plumber, pleasure, society, army.*   If you are in *doubt* whether a given *word* is a *noun,* try putting the *word* "my," or "this," or "large" (or some other *adjective*) in *front* of it.   If it makes *sense* in the *sentence* the *chances* are that the *word* in *question* is a *noun.*   [All the *words* in *italics* in this *paragraph* are *nouns.*]

Adjectives.   Adjectives are the words which delimit or give you *specific* information about the *various* nouns in a sentence.   They tell you size, color, weight, pleasantness, and many *other* qualities. *Such* words as *big, expensive, terrible, insipid, hot, delightful, ruddy, informative* are all *clear* adjectives.   If you are in *any* doubt whether a *certain* word is an adjective, add -er to it, or put the word "more" or "too" in front of it.   If it makes *good* sense in the sentence, and does not end in -ly, the chances are that it is an adjective.   (Pronoun-adjectives will be described under pronouns.)   [The adjectives in the *above* sentences are in italics.]

Articles.   There are only two kinds of articles in English, and they are easy to remember.   The definite article is "the" and the indefinite article is "a" or "an."

Verbs.   Verbs *are* the words that *tell* what action, or condition, or relationship *is going* on.   Such words as *was, is, jumps, achieved, keeps, buys, sells, has finished, run, will have, may, should pay, indicates are* all verb forms.   *Observe* that a verb *can be composed* of more than one word, as *will have* and *should pay,* above; these *are called* compound verbs.   As a rough guide for verbs, *try adding* -ed to the word you *are wondering* about, or *taking* off an -ed that *is* already there.   If it *makes* sense, the chances *are* that it *is* a verb.   (This *does* not always *work,* since the so-called strong or irregular verbs *make* forms by *changing* their middle vowels, like *spring, sprang, sprung.*)   [Verbs in this paragraph *are* in italics.]

Adverbs.   An adverb is a word that supplies additional information about a verb, an adjective, or another adverb.   It *usually* indicates time, or manner, or place, or degree.   It tells you

who, or *when,* or *where,* or to what degree things are happening.
Such words as *now, then, there, not, anywhere, never, somehow, always,
very,* and most words ending in -ly are *ordinarily* adverbs.   [Itali-
cized words are adverbs.]

Pronouns.   Pronouns are related to nouns, and take their place.
(Some grammars and dictionaries group pronouns and nouns
together as substantives.)   *They* mention persons, or objects of
any sort without actually giving their names.

There are several different kinds of pronouns.   (1) Personal
pronouns: by a grammatical convention *I, we, me, mine, us, ours*
are called first person pronouns, since *they* refer to the speaker;
you and *yours* are called second person pronouns, since *they* refer
to the person addressed; and *he, him, his, she, hers, they, them,
theirs* are called third person pronouns since *they* refer to the things
or persons discussed.   (2) Demonstrative pronouns: *this, that,
these, those.*   (3) Interrogative, or question, pronouns: *who, whom,
what, whose, which.*   (4) Relative pronouns, or pronouns *which*
refer back to something already mentioned: *who, whom, that,
which.*   (5) Others: *some, any, anyone, no one, other, whichever,
none,* etc.

Pronouns are difficult for *us,* since our categories are not as
clear as in some other languages, and *we* often use the same words
for *what* foreign-language speakers see as different situations.   First,
our interrogative and relative pronouns overlap, and must be
separated in translation.   The easiest way is to observe whether a
question is involved in the sentence.   Examples: "*Which* [int.] do
you like?"   "The inn, *which* [rel.] was not far from Tōkyō, had a
restaurant."   "*Who* [int.] is there?"   "*I* don't know *who* [int.]
was there."   "The porter *who* [rel.] took our bags was Number
2132."   *This* may seem to be a trivial difference to an English
speaker, but in some languages, like Japanese, *it* is very important.

Secondly, there is an overlap between pronouns and adjectives.
In some cases the word "this," for example, is a pronoun; in other
cases *it* is an adjective.   *This* also holds true for *his, its, her, any,*

none, other, some, that, these, those, and many other words. Note whether the word in question stands alone or is associated with another word. Examples: "*This* [pronoun] is *mine*." "This [adj.] taxi has no springs." Watch out for the word "that," which can be a pronoun or an adjective or a conjunction. And remember that "my," "your," "our," and "their" are always adjectives. [All pronouns in this section are in italics.]

Prepositions. Prepositions are the little words that introduce phrases that tell *about* condition, time, place, manner, association, degree, and similar topics. Such words as *with, in, beside, under, of, to, about, for,* and *upon* are prepositions. In English prepositions and adverbs overlap, but, as you will see *by* checking *in* your dictionary, there are usually differences *of* meaning *between* the two uses. [Prepositions *in* this paragraph are designated *by* italics.]

Conjunctions. Conjunctions are joining-words. They enable you to link words *or* groups of words into larger units, *and* to build compound *or* complex sentences out of simple sentence units. Such words as *and, but, although, or, unless,* are typical conjunctions. *Although* most conjunctions are easy enough to identify, the word "that" should be watched closely to see *that* it is not a pronoun *or* an adjective. [Conjunctions italicized.]

Words about Verbs

Verbs are responsible for most of the terminology in this short grammar. The basic terms are:

Conjugation. In many languages verbs fall into natural groups, according to the way they make their forms. These groupings are called conjugations, and are an aid to learning grammatical structure. Though it may seem difficult at first to speak of First and Second Conjugations, these are simply short ways of saying that verbs belonging to these classes make their forms according to certain consistent rules, which you can memorize.

Infinitive. This is the basic form which most dictionaries give for verbs in most languages, and in most languages it serves as the basis for classifying verbs. In English (with a very few exceptions) it has no special form. To find the infinitive for any English verb, just fill in this sentence: "I like to......... (walk, run, jump, swim, carry, disappear, etc.)." The infinitive in English is usually preceded by the word "to."

Tense. This is simply a formal way of saying "time." In English we think of time as being broken into three great segments: past, present, and future. Our verbs are assigned forms to indicate this division, and are further subdivided for shades of meaning. We subdivide the present time into the present (I walk) and present progressive (I am walking); the past into the simple past (I walked), progressive past (I was walking), perfect or present perfect (I have walked), past perfect or pluperfect (I had walked); and future into simple future (I shall walk) and future progressive (I shall be walking). These are the most common English tenses. Other languages, like Japanese, may not have exact counterparts.

Present Participles, Progressive Tenses. In English the present participle always ends in -*ing*. It can be used as a noun or an adjective in some situations, but its chief use is in *forming* the so-called progressive tenses. These are made by *putting* appropriate forms of the verb "to be" before a present participle: For "to walk" [an infinitive], for example, the present progressive would be: I am *walking*, you are *walking*, he is *walking*, etc.; past progressive, I was *walking*, you were *walking*, and so on. [Present participles are in italics.]

Past Participles, Perfect Tenses. The past participle in English is not *formed* as regularly as is the present participle. Sometimes it is *constructed* by adding -ed or -d to the present tense, as *walked, jumped, looked, received*; but there are many verbs where it is *formed* less regularly: *seen, been, swum, chosen, brought*. To find it, simply fill out the sentence "I have........." putting in the verb

form that your ear tells you is right for the particular verb.   If
you speak grammatically, you will have the past participle.

Past participles are sometimes used as adjectives: "Don't cry
over *spilt* milk."   Their most important use, however, is to form
the system of verb tenses that are *called* the perfect tenses: present
perfect (or perfect), past perfect (or pluperfect), etc.   In English
the present perfect tense is *formed* with the present tense of "to
have" and the past participle of a verb: I have *walked*, you have
run, he has *begun*, etc.   The past perfect is *formed*, similarly, with
the past tense of "to have" and the past participle: I had *walked*,
you had *run*, he had *begun*.   Most of the languages you are likely
to study have similar systems of perfect tenses, though they may
not be *formed* in exactly the same way as in English.   [Past
participles in italics.]

Preterit, Imperfect.   Many languages have more than one
verb tense for expressing an action that took place in the past.
They may use a perfect tense (which we have just covered), or a
preterit, or an imperfect.   English, although you may never have
thought about it, is one of these languages, for we can say "I have
spoken to him" [present perfect], or "I spoke to him" [simple
past], or "I was speaking to him" [past progressive].   These
sentences do not mean exactly the same thing, although the
differences are subtle, and are difficult to put into other
words.

While usage differs a little from language to language, if a
language has both a preterit and an imperfect, in general the
preterit corresponds to the English simple past (I ran, I swam,
I spoke), and the imperfect corresponds to the English past progressive (I was running, I was swimming, I was speaking).   If
you are curious to discover the mode of thought behind these
different tenses, try looking at the situation in terms of back-
ground-action and point-action.   One of the most important uses
of the imperfect is to provide a background against which a
single point-action can take place.   For example, "When I was
walking down the street [background, continued over a period of

time, hence past progressive or imperfect], I stubbed my toe [an instant or point of time, hence a simple past or preterit]."

Auxiliary Verbs. Auxiliary verbs are special words that are used to help other verbs make their forms. In English, for example, we use forms of the verb "to have" to make our perfect tenses: I have seen, you had come, he has been, etc. We also use "shall" or "will" to make our future tenses: I shall pay, you will see, etc. French, German, Spanish, and Italian also make use of auxiliary verbs, but although the same general concept is present, the use of auxiliaries differs very much from one language to another, and you must learn the practice for each language.

Passive. In some languages, like Latin, there is a strong feeling that an action or thing that is taking place can be expressed in two different ways. One can say, A does-something-to B, which is "active"; or B is-having-something-done-to-him by A, which is "passive." We do not have a strong feeling for this classification of experience in English, but the following examples should indicate the difference between an active and a passive verb: Active: "John is building a house." Passive: "A house is being built by John." Active: "The steamer carried the cotton to England." Passive: "The cotton was carried by the steamer to England." Bear in mind that the formation of passive verbs and the situations where they can be used vary enormously from language to language. This is one situation where you usually cannot translate English word for word into another language and make sense.

Miscellaneous Terms

Comparative, Superlative. These two terms are used with adjectives and adverbs. They indicate the degree of strength within the meaning of the word. Faster, better, earlier, newer, more rapid, more detailed, more suitable are examples of the comparative in adjectives, while more rapidly, more recently, more suitably are comparatives for adverbs. In most cases, as you have seen, the comparative uses -er or "more" for an adjective, and "more" for an adverb. Superlatives are those forms which end in -est or have "most" placed before them for adjectives, and "most" prefixed for adverbs: most intelligent, earliest, most rapidly, most suitably.

Idiom. An idiom is an expression that is peculiar to a language, the meaning of which is not the same as the literal meaning of the individual words composing it. Idioms, as a rule, cannot be translated word by word into another language. Examples of English idioms: "*Take it easy.*" "Don't *beat around the bush.*" "It *turned out* to be *a Dutch treat.*" "Can you *tell time* in Italian?"

The Parts of the Sentence

Subject, Predicate. In grammar *every complete sentence* contains two basic parts, the subject and the predicate. *The subject,* if *we* state the terms most simply, is the thing, person, or activity talked about. *It* can be a noun, a pronoun, or something *that* serves as a noun. *A subject* would include, in a typical case, a noun, the articles or adjectives *which* are associated with it, and perhaps phrases. Note that in complex sentences, *each part* may have its own subject. [*The subjects of the sentences above* have been italicized.]

The predicate *talks about the subject.* In a formal sentence the predicate *includes a verb, its adverbs, predicate adjectives, phrases, and objects*—whatever *happens to be present.* A predicate adjective *is an adjective* which *happens to be in the predicate after a form of the verb to be.* Example: "Apples *are red.*" [Predicates *are in italics.*]

In the following simple sentences subjects are in italics, predicates in italics and underlined. "*Green apples are bad for your digestion.*" "When *I go to Japan, I always stop in Tōkyō.*" "*The man with the handbag is travelling to Kōbe.*"

Direct and Indirect Objects. Some verbs (called transitive verbs) take direct and/or indirect objects in their predicates; other verbs (called intransitive verbs) do not take objects of any sort. In English, except for pronouns, objects do not have any special forms, but in languages which have case forms or more pronoun forms than English, objects can be troublesome.

The direct object is the person, thing, quality, or matter that the verb directs *its action* upon. It can be a pronoun, or a noun, perhaps accompanied by an article and/or adjectives. The direct object always directly follows *its verb*, except when there is also an indirect object present, which comes between the verb and the object. Prepositions do not go before direct objects. Examples: "The cook threw *green onions* into the stew." "The border guards will want to see *your passport* tomorrow." "Give *it* to me." "Please give me *a glass of red wine*." [We have placed *direct objects* in this paragraph in italics.]

The indirect object, as grammars will tell *you*, is the person or thing for or to whom the action is taking place. It can be a pronoun or a noun with or without article and adjectives. In most cases the words "to" or "for" can be inserted before it, if they are not already there. Examples: "Please tell *me* the time." "I wrote *her* a letter from Ōsaka." "We sent *Mr. Tanizaki* fifty yen." "We gave *the most energetic guide* a large tip." [Indirect objects are in italics.]

Clauses: Independent, Dependent, Relative. Clauses are the largest components/*that go to make up sentences.*/ Each clause, in classical grammar, is a combination of subject and predicate./ *If a sentence has one subject and one predicate,*/ it is a one-clause sentence./*If it has two or more subjects and predicates,*/ it is a sentence of two or more clauses./

There are two kinds of clauses: independent (principal) and dependent (subordinate) clauses./ An independent clause can stand alone;/it can form a logical, complete sentence./ A dependent clause is a clause/*that cannot stand alone*;/it must have another clause with it to complete it./

A sentence containing a single clause is called a simple sentence./ A sentence with two or more clauses may be either a complex or a compound sentence./ A compound sentence contains two or more independent clauses,/and/these independent clauses are joined together with and or but./ A complex sentence is a sentence/*which contains both independent and dependent clauses.*/

A relative clause is a clause/*which begins with a relative pronoun: who, whom, that, which.*/ It is by definition a dependent clause,/ *since it cannot stand by itself.*

In English these terms are not very important except for rhetorical analysis,/*since all clauses are treated very much the same in grammar and syntax.* In some foreign languages, like Japanese, however, these concepts are important,/and they must be understood,/*since all clauses are not treated alike.* [Each clause in this section has been isolated by slashes./ Dependent clauses have been placed in italics;/independent clauses have not been marked./]

Special Terms Describing Japanese Grammar

In our description of Japanese grammar we have used a few special terms which may not be familiar to the reader. These terms have been explained within the text as they arose, but we shall repeat brief definitions here. For more detail consult the pages indicated.

Stems. In some languages, like Japanese, Latin, or classical Greek, where endings or prefixes are used to make new forms, there is often a basic element (which cannot normally be used by itself) to which the endings or prefixes are added. This basic element is called a stem. The concept of the stem is not too significant in the Germanic portion of English, but traces of it can be found in many of the words and concepts borrowed from Latin and Greek. In the words lexicon, lexical, lexically, lexicographer the form lexic- is a stem; it cannot be used by itself, but it can be used to form a range of words (or ideas) by adding new material.

In Japanese, verbs and adjectives are best analyzed in terms of stems. The ultimate form to which you can go in a verb is the so-called basic stem (see page 37), which is used as a substructure for all other stems and forms. We describe three other stems in this brief survey: the combining stem, which is used when you join one verb to another or make ordinary tenses (see page 39); the

negative stem, which is used to make negative forms (see page 52);
and the conditional stem, which we have mentioned only for
recognition (see page 88).

Adjectives, for the purpose of this brief survey, have only one
stem, a basic stem, from which all other forms are made (see page
63).

Probable Forms.   Verbs and adjectives have sets of forms which
are used to indicate probability, doubt, and similar areas of meaning which we express by more complex constructions in English.
"We shall probably come," "I think we shall come," and similar
ideas are expressed by special forms which are made as regularly
as other verb forms (see page 47).

Final and Medial Forms.   Certain verb and adjective forms can
be used without other forms to complete them; they are there-
by independent verbs upon which complete sentences are
founded.   According to the genius of Japanese, these forms are
placed in final position: at the end of a sentence, at the end of a
clause, or at the end of modifying material.   These forms include
present, present progressive, past, past progressive, probable and
probable progressive.   Certain other forms, however, do not
have sufficient strength to be used without other verbs to complete
their sense.   These forms are placed within the sentence, and
cannot appear as a final element.   Such forms include the true
verb or adjective conditional, the participle if used without a com-
pleting form, the various stems, and for the adjective the continuative or suspending form (see page 68).   (This, of course,
refers to exact speech; colloquially, exceptions may be made.)

This may seem like an alien concept, but actually we have the
same practice, though to a somewhat lesser extent, in English.
A sentence that contains only a present participle or an infinitive
or a past participle is not considered a complete sentence.   Example: "Walking down the street . . .," "To be or not to be . . .,"
"Gone out of my life. . . ."

Postpositions and Particles. Particles are small units of speech (found in certain languages like Japanese, and to a lesser extent, classical Greek) which indicate relationships within a sentence, but do not coincide with the basic English parts of speech. In Japanese they perform the offices of prepositions and conjunctions, and also serve as pointers to show material that has been set off from the rest of the sentence and to indicate subjects and direct objects. Since they are always placed after the material they govern, they are also called postpositions.

Classifier. In Japanese and Chinese objects that are counted are normally listed according to certain units, which vary according to the object itself. This is best understood by our comparable (though much less important) English practice: two sheets of paper, five head of cattle, three sticks of wood, etc. These terms sheets, head, sticks have nothing to do with quantity or with special type of material; they are simply a convention in counting. But while classifiers are exceptional in English, they are extremely important in Japanese.

Index

The following abbreviations have been used in this index: *conj.* for conjunction and *def.* for definition. Japanese words appear in *italics* and their English equivalents in parentheses. Where no true equivalent is possible, as in the case of some particles, the material in parentheses is not a translation, but an identification, such as "particle" or "nominalizer."

A CATALOG OF SELECTED
DOVER BOOKS
IN ALL FIELDS OF INTEREST

A CATALOG OF SELECTED DOVER
BOOKS IN ALL FIELDS OF INTEREST

DRAWINGS OF REMBRANDT, edited by Seymour Slive. Updated Lippmann, Hofstede de Groot edition, with definitive scholarly apparatus. All portraits, biblical sketches, landscapes, nudes. Oriental figures, classical studies, together with selection of work by followers. 550 illustrations. Total of 630pp. 9⅛ × 12¼.
21485-0, 21486-9 Pa., Two-vol. set $25.00

GHOST AND HORROR STORIES OF AMBROSE BIERCE, Ambrose Bierce. 24 tales vividly imagined, strangely prophetic, and decades ahead of their time in technical skill: "The Damned Thing," "An Inhabitant of Carcosa," "The Eyes of the Panther," "Moxon's Master," and 20 more. 199pp. 5⅜ × 8½. 20767-6 Pa. $3.95

ETHICAL WRITINGS OF MAIMONIDES, Maimonides. Most significant ethical works of great medieval sage, newly translated for utmost precision, readability. Laws Concerning Character Traits, Eight Chapters, more. 192pp. 5⅜ × 8½.
24522-5 Pa. $4.50

THE EXPLORATION OF THE COLORADO RIVER AND ITS CANYONS, J. W. Powell. Full text of Powell's 1,000-mile expedition down the fabled Colorado in 1869. Superb account of terrain, geology, vegetation, Indians, famine, mutiny, treacherous rapids, mighty canyons, during exploration of last unknown part of continental U.S. 400pp. 5⅜ × 8½. 20094-9 Pa. $6.95

HISTORY OF PHILOSOPHY, Julián Marías. Clearest one-volume history on the market. Every major philosopher and dozens of others, to Existentialism and later. 505pp. 5⅜ × 8½. 21739-6 Pa. $9.95

ALL ABOUT LIGHTNING, Martin A. Uman. Highly readable non-technical survey of nature and causes of lightning, thunderstorms, ball lightning, St. Elmo's Fire, much more. Illustrated. 192pp. 5⅜ × 8½. 25237-X Pa. $5.95

SAILING ALONE AROUND THE WORLD, Captain Joshua Slocum. First man to sail around the world, alone, in small boat. One of great feats of seamanship told in delightful manner. 67 illustrations. 294pp. 5⅜ × 8½. 20326-3 Pa. $4.95

LETTERS AND NOTES ON THE MANNERS, CUSTOMS AND CONDITIONS OF THE NORTH AMERICAN INDIANS, George Catlin. Classic account of life among Plains Indians: ceremonies, hunt, warfare, etc. 312 plates. 572pp. of text. 6⅛ × 9¼. 22118-0, 22119-9 Pa. Two-vol. set $15.90

ALASKA: The Harriman Expedition, 1899, John Burroughs, John Muir, et al. Informative, engrossing accounts of two-month, 9,000-mile expedition. Native peoples, wildlife, forests, geography, salmon industry, glaciers, more. Profusely illustrated. 240 black-and-white line drawings. 124 black-and-white photographs. 3 maps. Index. 576pp. 5⅜ × 8½. 25109-8 Pa. $11.95

CATALOG OF DOVER BOOKS

THE BOOK OF BEASTS: Being a Translation from a Latin Bestiary of the Twelfth Century, T. H. White. Wonderful catalog real and fanciful beasts: manticore, griffin, phoenix, amphivius, jaculus, many more. White's witty erudite commentary on scientific, historical aspects. Fascinating glimpse of medieval mind. Illustrated. 296pp. 5⅜ × 8¼. (Available in U.S. only) 24609-4 Pa. $5.95

FRANK LLOYD WRIGHT: ARCHITECTURE AND NATURE With 160 Illustrations, Donald Hoffmann. Profusely illustrated study of influence of nature—especially prairie—on Wright's designs for Fallingwater, Robie House, Guggenheim Museum, other masterpieces. 96pp. 9¼ × 10¾. 25098-9 Pa. $7.95

FRANK LLOYD WRIGHT'S FALLINGWATER, Donald Hoffmann. Wright's famous waterfall house: planning and construction of organic idea. History of site, owners, Wright's personal involvement. Photographs of various stages of building. Preface by Edgar Kaufmann, Jr. 100 illustrations. 112pp. 9¼ × 10.
23671-4 Pa. $7.95

YEARS WITH FRANK LLOYD WRIGHT: Apprentice to Genius, Edgar Tafel. Insightful memoir by a former apprentice presents a revealing portrait of Wright the man, the inspired teacher, the greatest American architect. 372 black-and-white illustrations. Preface. Index. vi + 228pp. 8¼ × 11. 24801-1 Pa. $9.95

THE STORY OF KING ARTHUR AND HIS KNIGHTS, Howard Pyle. Enchanting version of King Arthur fable has delighted generations with imaginative narratives of exciting adventures and unforgettable illustrations by the author. 41 illustrations. xviii + 313pp. 6⅛ × 9¼. 21445-1 Pa. $6.50

THE GODS OF THE EGYPTIANS, E. A. Wallis Budge. Thorough coverage of numerous gods of ancient Egypt by foremost Egyptologist. Information on evolution of cults, rites and gods; the cult of Osiris; the Book of the Dead and its rites; the sacred animals and birds; Heaven and Hell; and more. 956pp. 6⅛ × 9¼.
22055-9, 22056-7 Pa., Two-vol. set $21.90

A THEOLOGICO-POLITICAL TREATISE, Benedict Spinoza. Also contains unfinished *Political Treatise*. Great classic on religious liberty, theory of government on common consent. R. Elwes translation. Total of 421pp. 5⅜ × 8½.
20249-6 Pa. $6.95

INCIDENTS OF TRAVEL IN CENTRAL AMERICA, CHIAPAS, AND YUCATAN, John L. Stephens. Almost single-handed discovery of Maya culture; exploration of ruined cities, monuments, temples; customs of Indians. 115 drawings. 892pp. 5⅜ × 8½. 22404-X, 22405-8 Pa., Two-vol. set $15.90

LOS CAPRICHOS, Francisco Goya. 80 plates of wild, grotesque monsters and caricatures. Prado manuscript included. 183pp. 6⅝ × 9⅜. 22384-1 Pa. $4.95

AUTOBIOGRAPHY: The Story of My Experiments with Truth, Mohandas K. Gandhi. Not hagiography, but Gandhi in his own words. Boyhood, legal studies, purification, the growth of the Satyagraha (nonviolent protest) movement. Critical, inspiring work of the man who freed India. 480pp. 5⅜ × 8½. (Available in U.S. only)
24593-4 Pa. $6.95

ILLUSTRATED DICTIONARY OF HISTORIC ARCHITECTURE, edited by Cyril M. Harris. Extraordinary compendium of clear, concise definitions for over 5,000 important architectural terms complemented by over 2,000 line drawings. Covers full spectrum of architecture from ancient ruins to 20th-century Modernism. Preface. 592pp. 7½ × 9⅝. 24444-X Pa. $15.95

THE NIGHT BEFORE CHRISTMAS, Clement Moore. Full text, and woodcuts from original 1848 book. Also critical, historical material. 19 illustrations. 40pp. 4⅝ × 6. 22797-9 Pa. $2.50

THE LESSON OF JAPANESE ARCHITECTURE: 165 Photographs, Jiro Harada. Memorable gallery of 165 photographs taken in the 1930's of exquisite Japanese homes of the well-to-do and historic buildings. 13 line diagrams. 192pp. 8⅜ × 11¼. 24778-3 Pa. $8.95

THE AUTOBIOGRAPHY OF CHARLES DARWIN AND SELECTED LETTERS, edited by Francis Darwin. The fascinating life of eccentric genius composed of an intimate memoir by Darwin (intended for his children); commentary by his son, Francis; hundreds of fragments from notebooks, journals, papers; and letters to and from Lyell, Hooker, Huxley, Wallace and Henslow. xi + 365pp. 5⅜ × 8. 20479-0 Pa. $6.95

WONDERS OF THE SKY: Observing Rainbows, Comets, Eclipses, the Stars and Other Phenomena, Fred Schaaf. Charming, easy-to-read poetic guide to all manner of celestial events visible to the naked eye. Mock suns, glories, Belt of Venus, more. Illustrated. 299pp. 5¼ × 8¼. 24402-4 Pa. $7.95

BURNHAM'S CELESTIAL HANDBOOK, Robert Burnham, Jr. Thorough guide to the stars beyond our solar system. Exhaustive treatment. Alphabetical by constellation: Andromeda to Cetus in Vol. 1; Chamaeleon to Orion in Vol. 2; and Pavo to Vulpecula in Vol. 3. Hundreds of illustrations. Index in Vol. 3. 2,000pp. 6⅛ × 9¼. 23567-X, 23568-8, 23673-0 Pa., Three-vol. set $38.85

STAR NAMES: Their Lore and Meaning, Richard Hinckley Allen. Fascinating history of names various cultures have given to constellations and literary and folkloristic uses that have been made of stars. Indexes to subjects. Arabic and Greek names. Biblical references. Bibliography. 563pp. 5⅜ × 8½. 21079-0 Pa. $7.95

THIRTY YEARS THAT SHOOK PHYSICS: The Story of Quantum Theory, George Gamow. Lucid, accessible introduction to influential theory of energy and matter. Careful explanations of Dirac's anti-particles, Bohr's model of the atom, much more. 12 plates. Numerous drawings. 240pp. 5⅜ × 8½. 24895-X Pa. $5.95

CHINESE DOMESTIC FURNITURE IN PHOTOGRAPHS AND MEASURED DRAWINGS, Gustav Ecke. A rare volume, now affordably priced for antique collectors, furniture buffs and art historians. Detailed review of styles ranging from early Shang to late Ming. Unabridged republication. 161 black-and-white drawings, photos. Total of 224pp. 8⅜ × 11¼. (Available in U.S. only) 25171-3 Pa. $12.95

VINCENT VAN GOGH: A Biography, Julius Meier-Graefe. Dynamic, penetrating study of artist's life, relationship with brother, Theo, painting techniques, travels, more. Readable, engrossing. 160pp. 5⅜ × 8½. (Available in U.S. only) 25253-1 Pa. $3.95

HOW TO WRITE, Gertrude Stein. Gertrude Stein claimed anyone could understand her unconventional writing—here are clues to help. Fascinating improvisations, language experiments, explanations illuminate Stein's craft and the art of writing. Total of 414pp. 4⅝ × 6⅜. 23144-5 Pa. $5.95

ADVENTURES AT SEA IN THE GREAT AGE OF SAIL: Five Firsthand Narratives, edited by Elliot Snow. Rare true accounts of exploration, whaling, shipwreck, fierce natives, trade, shipboard life, more. 33 illustrations. Introduction. 353pp. 5⅜ × 8½. 25177-2 Pa. $7.95

THE HERBAL OR GENERAL HISTORY OF PLANTS, John Gerard. Classic descriptions of about 2,850 plants—with over 2,700 illustrations—includes Latin and English names, physical descriptions, varieties, time and place of growth, more. 2,706 illustrations. xlv + 1,678pp. 8½ × 12¼. 23147-X Cloth. $75.00

DOROTHY AND THE WIZARD IN OZ, L. Frank Baum. Dorothy and the Wizard visit the center of the Earth, where people are vegetables, glass houses grow and Oz characters reappear. Classic sequel to *Wizard of Oz*. 256pp. 5⅜ × 8. 24714-7 Pa. $4.95

SONGS OF EXPERIENCE: Facsimile Reproduction with 26 Plates in Full Color, William Blake. This facsimile of Blake's original "Illuminated Book" reproduces 26 full-color plates from a rare 1826 edition. Includes "The Tyger," "London," "Holy Thursday," and other immortal poems. 26 color plates. Printed text of poems. 48pp. 5¼ × 7. 24636-1 Pa. $3.50

SONGS OF INNOCENCE, William Blake. The first and most popular of Blake's famous "Illuminated Books," in a facsimile edition reproducing all 31 brightly colored plates. Additional printed text of each poem. 64pp. 5¼ × 7. 22764-2 Pa. $3.50

PRECIOUS STONES, Max Bauer. Classic, thorough study of diamonds, rubies, emeralds, garnets, etc.: physical character, occurrence, properties, use, similar topics. 20 plates, 8 in color. 94 figures. 659pp. 6⅛ × 9¼. 21910-0, 21911-9 Pa., Two-vol. set $15.90

ENCYCLOPEDIA OF VICTORIAN NEEDLEWORK, S. F. A. Caulfeild and Blanche Saward. Full, precise descriptions of stitches, techniques for dozens of needlecrafts—most exhaustive reference of its kind. Over 800 figures. Total of 679pp. 8⅛ × 11. Two volumes. Vol. 1 22800-2 Pa. $11.95
Vol. 2 22801-0 Pa. $11.95

THE MARVELOUS LAND OF OZ, L. Frank Baum. Second Oz book, the Scarecrow and Tin Woodman are back with hero named Tip, Oz magic. 136 illustrations. 287pp. 5⅜ × 8½. 20692-0 Pa. $5.95

WILD FOWL DECOYS, Joel Barber. Basic book on the subject, by foremost authority and collector. Reveals history of decoy making and rigging, place in American culture, different kinds of decoys, how to make them, and how to use them. 140 plates. 156pp. 7⅞ × 10¾. 20011-6 Pa. $8.95

HISTORY OF LACE, Mrs. Bury Palliser. Definitive, profusely illustrated chronicle of lace from earliest times to late 19th century. Laces of Italy, Greece, England, France, Belgium, etc. Landmark of needlework scholarship. 266 illustrations. 672pp. 6⅛ × 9¼. 24742-2 Pa. $14.95

ILLUSTRATED GUIDE TO SHAKER FURNITURE, Robert Meader. All furniture and appurtenances, with much on unknown local styles. 235 photos. 146pp. 9 × 12. 22819-3 Pa. $7.95

WHALE SHIPS AND WHALING: A Pictorial Survey, George Francis Dow. Over 200 vintage engravings, drawings, photographs of barks, brigs, cutters, other vessels. Also harpoons, lances, whaling guns, many other artifacts. Comprehensive text by foremost authority. 207 black-and-white illustrations. 288pp. 6 × 9.
24808-9 Pa. $8.95

THE BERTRAMS, Anthony Trollope. Powerful portrayal of blind self-will and thwarted ambition includes one of Trollope's most heartrending love stories. 497pp. 5⅜ × 8½. 25119-5 Pa. $9.95

ADVENTURES WITH A HAND LENS, Richard Headstrom. Clearly written guide to observing and studying flowers and grasses, fish scales, moth and insect wings, egg cases, buds, feathers, seeds, leaf scars, moss, molds, ferns, common crystals, etc.—all with an ordinary, inexpensive magnifying glass. 209 exact line drawings aid in your discoveries. 220pp. 5⅜ × 8½. 23330-8 Pa. $4.95

RODIN ON ART AND ARTISTS, Auguste Rodin. Great sculptor's candid, wide-ranging comments on meaning of art; great artists; relation of sculpture to poetry, painting, music; philosophy of life, more. 76 superb black-and-white illustrations of Rodin's sculpture, drawings and prints. 119pp. 8⅜ × 11¼. 24487-3 Pa. $6.95

FIFTY CLASSIC FRENCH FILMS, 1912–1982: A Pictorial Record, Anthony Slide. Memorable stills from Grand Illusion, Beauty and the Beast, Hiroshima, Mon Amour, many more. Credits, plot synopses, reviews, etc. 160pp. 8¼ × 11.
25256-6 Pa. $11.95

THE PRINCIPLES OF PSYCHOLOGY, William James. Famous long course complete, unabridged. Stream of thought, time perception, memory, experimental methods; great work decades ahead of its time. 94 figures. 1,391pp. 5⅜ × 8½.
20381-6, 20382-4 Pa., Two-vol. set $23.90

BODIES IN A BOOKSHOP, R. T. Campbell. Challenging mystery of blackmail and murder with ingenious plot and superbly drawn characters. In the best tradition of British suspense fiction. 192pp. 5⅜ × 8½. 24720-1 Pa. $3.95

CALLAS: PORTRAIT OF A PRIMA DONNA, George Jellinek. Renowned commentator on the musical scene chronicles incredible career and life of the most controversial, fascinating, influential operatic personality of our time. 64 black-and-white photographs. 416pp. 5⅜ × 8¼. 25047-4 Pa. $8.95

GEOMETRY, RELATIVITY AND THE FOURTH DIMENSION, Rudolph Rucker. Exposition of fourth dimension, concepts of relativity as Flatland characters continue adventures. Popular, easily followed yet accurate, profound. 141 illustrations. 133pp. 5⅜ × 8½. 23400-2 Pa. $3.95

HOUSEHOLD STORIES BY THE BROTHERS GRIMM, with pictures by Walter Crane. 53 classic stories—Rumpelstiltskin, Rapunzel, Hansel and Gretel, the Fisherman and his Wife, Snow White, Tom Thumb, Sleeping Beauty, Cinderella, and so much more—lavishly illustrated with original 19th century drawings. 114 illustrations. x + 269pp. 5⅜ × 8½. 21080-4 Pa. $4.95

SUNDIALS, Albert Waugh. Far and away the best, most thorough coverage of ideas, mathematics concerned, types, construction, adjusting anywhere. Over 100 illustrations. 230pp. 5⅜ × 8½. 22947-5 Pa. $4.95

PICTURE HISTORY OF THE NORMANDIE: With 190 Illustrations, Frank O. Braynard. Full story of legendary French ocean liner: Art Deco interiors, design innovations, furnishings, celebrities, maiden voyage, tragic fire, much more. Extensive text. 144pp. 8⅞ × 11¾. 25257-4 Pa. $9.95

THE FIRST AMERICAN COOKBOOK: A Facsimile of "American Cookery," 1796, Amelia Simmons. Facsimile of the first American-written cookbook published in the United States contains authentic recipes for colonial favorites—pumpkin pudding, winter squash pudding, spruce beer, Indian slapjacks, and more. Introductory Essay and Glossary of colonial cooking terms. 80pp. 5⅜ × 8½. 24710-4 Pa. $3.50

101 PUZZLES IN THOUGHT AND LOGIC, C. R. Wylie, Jr. Solve murders and robberies, find out which fishermen are liars, how a blind man could possibly identify a color—purely by your own reasoning! 107pp. 5⅜ × 8½. 20367-0 Pa. $2.50

THE BOOK OF WORLD-FAMOUS MUSIC—CLASSICAL, POPULAR AND FOLK, James J. Fuld. Revised and enlarged republication of landmark work in musico-bibliography. Full information about nearly 1,000 songs and compositions including first lines of music and lyrics. New supplement. Index. 800pp. 5⅜ × 8¼. 24857-7 Pa. $14.95

ANTHROPOLOGY AND MODERN LIFE, Franz Boas. Great anthropologist's classic treatise on race and culture. Introduction by Ruth Bunzel. Only inexpensive paperback edition. 255pp. 5⅜ × 8½. 25245-0 Pa. $5.95

THE TALE OF PETER RABBIT, Beatrix Potter. The inimitable Peter's terrifying adventure in Mr. McGregor's garden, with all 27 wonderful, full-color Potter illustrations. 55pp. 4¼ × 5½. (Available in U.S. only) 22827-4 Pa. $1.75

THREE PROPHETIC SCIENCE FICTION NOVELS, H. G. Wells. *When the Sleeper Wakes, A Story of the Days to Come* and *The Time Machine* (full version). 335pp. 5⅜ × 8½. (Available in U.S. only) 20605-X Pa. $6.95

APICIUS COOKERY AND DINING IN IMPERIAL ROME, edited and translated by Joseph Dommers Vehling. Oldest known cookbook in existence offers readers a clear picture of what foods Romans ate, how they prepared them, etc. 49 illustrations. 301pp. 6⅛ × 9¼. 23563-7 Pa. $7.95

SHAKESPEARE LEXICON AND QUOTATION DICTIONARY, Alexander Schmidt. Full definitions, locations, shades of meaning of every word in plays and poems. More than 50,000 exact quotations. 1,485pp. 6½ × 9¼. 22726-X, 22727-8 Pa., Two-vol. set $29.90

THE WORLD'S GREAT SPEECHES, edited by Lewis Copeland and Lawrence W. Lamm. Vast collection of 278 speeches from Greeks to 1970. Powerful and effective models; unique look at history. 842pp. 5⅜ × 8½. 20468-5 Pa. $11.95

THE BLUE FAIRY BOOK, Andrew Lang. The first, most famous collection, with many familiar tales: Little Red Riding Hood, Aladdin and the Wonderful Lamp, Puss in Boots, Sleeping Beauty, Hansel and Gretel, Rumpelstiltskin; 37 in all. 138 illustrations. 390pp. 5⅜ × 8½.   21437-0 Pa. $6.95

THE STORY OF THE CHAMPIONS OF THE ROUND TABLE, Howard Pyle. Sir Launcelot, Sir Tristram and Sir Percival in spirited adventures of love and triumph retold in Pyle's inimitable style. 50 drawings, 31 full-page. xviii + 329pp. 6½ × 9¼.   21883-X Pa. $6.95

AUDUBON AND HIS JOURNALS, Maria Audubon. Unmatched two-volume portrait of the great artist, naturalist and author contains his journals, an excellent biography by his granddaughter, expert annotations by the noted ornithologist, Dr. Elliott Coues, and 37 superb illustrations. Total of 1,200pp. 5⅜ × 8.
Vol. I 25143-8 Pa. $8.95
Vol. II 25144-6 Pa. $8.95

GREAT DINOSAUR HUNTERS AND THEIR DISCOVERIES, Edwin H. Colbert. Fascinating, lavishly illustrated chronicle of dinosaur research, 1820's to 1960. Achievements of Cope, Marsh, Brown, Buckland, Mantell, Huxley, many others. 384pp. 5¼ × 8¼.   24701-5 Pa. $7.95

THE TASTEMAKERS, Russell Lynes. Informal, illustrated social history of American taste 1850's–1950's. First popularized categories Highbrow, Lowbrow, Middlebrow. 129 illustrations. New (1979) afterword. 384pp. 6 × 9.
23993-4 Pa. $8.95

DOUBLE CROSS PURPOSES, Ronald A. Knox. A treasure hunt in the Scottish Highlands, an old map, unidentified corpse, surprise discoveries keep reader guessing in this cleverly intricate tale of financial skullduggery. 2 black-and-white maps. 320pp. 5⅜ × 8½. (Available in U.S. only)   25032-6 Pa. $5.95

AUTHENTIC VICTORIAN DECORATION AND ORNAMENTATION IN FULL COLOR: 46 Plates from "Studies in Design," Christopher Dresser. Superb full-color lithographs reproduced from rare original portfolio of a major Victorian designer. 48pp. 9¼ × 12¼.   25083-0 Pa. $7.95

PRIMITIVE ART, Franz Boas. Remains the best text ever prepared on subject, thoroughly discussing Indian, African, Asian, Australian, and, especially, North-ern American primitive art. Over 950 illustrations show ceramics, masks, totem poles, weapons, textiles, paintings, much more. 376pp. 5⅜ × 8.   20025-6 Pa. $6.95

SIDELIGHTS ON RELATIVITY, Albert Einstein. Unabridged republication of two lectures delivered by the great physicist in 1920–21. *Ether and Relativity* and *Geometry and Experience*. Elegant ideas in non-mathematical form, accessible to intelligent layman. vi + 56pp. 5⅜ × 8½.   24511-X Pa. $2.95

THE WIT AND HUMOR OF OSCAR WILDE, edited by Alvin Redman. More than 1,000 ripostes, paradoxes, wisecracks: Work is the curse of the drinking classes, I can resist everything except temptation, etc. 258pp. 5⅜ × 8½.   20602-5 Pa. $4.50

ADVENTURES WITH A MICROSCOPE, Richard Headstrom. 59 adventures with clothing fibers, protozoa, ferns and lichens, roots and leaves, much more. 142 illustrations. 232pp. 5⅜ × 8½.   23471-1 Pa. $3.95

PLANTS OF THE BIBLE, Harold N. Moldenke and Alma L. Moldenke. Standard reference to all 230 plants mentioned in Scriptures. Latin name, biblical reference, uses, modern identity, much more. Unsurpassed encyclopedic resource for scholars, botanists, nature lovers, students of Bible. Bibliography. Indexes. 123 black-and-white illustrations. 384pp. 6 × 9. 25069-5 Pa. $8.95

FAMOUS AMERICAN WOMEN: A Biographical Dictionary from Colonial Times to the Present, Robert McHenry, ed. From Pocahontas to Rosa Parks, 1,035 distinguished American women documented in separate biographical entries. Accurate, up-to-date data, numerous categories, spans 400 years. Indices. 493pp. 6½ × 9¼. 24523-3 Pa. $9.95

THE FABULOUS INTERIORS OF THE GREAT OCEAN LINERS IN HISTORIC PHOTOGRAPHS, William H. Miller, Jr. Some 200 superb photographs capture exquisite interiors of world's great "floating palaces"—1890's to 1980's: *Titanic, Ile de France, Queen Elizabeth, United States, Europa,* more. Approx. 200 black-and-white photographs. Captions. Text. Introduction. 160pp. 8⅞ × 11¾. 24756-2 Pa. $9.95

THE GREAT LUXURY LINERS, 1927–1954: A Photographic Record, William H. Miller, Jr. Nostalgic tribute to heyday of ocean liners. 186 photos of Ile de France, Normandie, Leviathan, Queen Elizabeth, United States, many others. Interior and exterior views. Introduction. Captions. 160pp. 9 × 12. 24056-8 Pa. $10.95

A NATURAL HISTORY OF THE DUCKS, John Charles Phillips. Great landmark of ornithology offers complete detailed coverage of nearly 200 species and subspecies of ducks: gadwall, sheldrake, merganser, pintail, many more. 74 full-color plates, 102 black-and-white. Bibliography. Total of 1,920pp. 8⅜ × 11¼. 25141-1, 25142-X Cloth. Two-vol. set $100.00

THE SEAWEED HANDBOOK: An Illustrated Guide to Seaweeds from North Carolina to Canada, Thomas F. Lee. Concise reference covers 78 species. Scientific and common names, habitat, distribution, more. Finding keys for easy identification. 224pp. 5⅜ × 8½. 25215-9 Pa. $5.95

THE TEN BOOKS OF ARCHITECTURE: The 1755 Leoni Edition, Leon Battista Alberti. Rare classic helped introduce the glories of ancient architecture to the Renaissance. 68 black-and-white plates. 336pp. 8⅜ × 11¼. 25239-6 Pa. $14.95

MISS MACKENZIE, Anthony Trollope. Minor masterpieces by Victorian master unmasks many truths about life in 19th-century England. First inexpensive edition in years. 392pp. 5⅜ × 8½. 25201-9 Pa. $7.95

THE RIME OF THE ANCIENT MARINER, Gustave Doré, Samuel Taylor Coleridge. Dramatic engravings considered by many to be his greatest work. The terrifying space of the open sea, the storms and whirlpools of an unknown ocean, the ice of Antarctica, more—all rendered in a powerful, chilling manner. Full text. 38 plates. 77pp. 9¼ × 12. 22305-1 Pa. $4.95

THE EXPEDITIONS OF ZEBULON MONTGOMERY PIKE, Zebulon Montgomery Pike. Fascinating first-hand accounts (1805–6) of exploration of Mississippi River, Indian wars, capture by Spanish dragoons, much more. 1,088pp. 5⅜ × 8½. 25254-X, 25255-8 Pa. Two-vol. set $23.90

A CONCISE HISTORY OF PHOTOGRAPHY: Third Revised Edition, Helmut Gernsheim. Best one-volume history—camera obscura, photochemistry, daguerreotypes, evolution of cameras, film, more. Also artistic aspects—landscape, portraits, fine art, etc. 281 black-and-white photographs. 26 in color. 176pp. 8⅜ × 11¼. 25128-4 Pa. $13.95

THE DORÉ BIBLE ILLUSTRATIONS, Gustave Doré. 241 detailed plates from the Bible: the Creation scenes, Adam and Eve, Flood, Babylon, battle sequences, life of Jesus, etc. Each plate is accompanied by the verses from the King James version of the Bible. 241pp. 9 × 12. 23004-X Pa. $8.95

HUGGER-MUGGER IN THE LOUVRE, Elliot Paul. Second Homer Evans mystery-comedy. Theft at the Louvre involves sleuth in hilarious, madcap caper. "A knockout."—Books. 336pp. 5⅜ × 8½. 25185-3 Pa. $5.95

FLATLAND, E. A. Abbott. Intriguing and enormously popular science-fiction classic explores the complexities of trying to survive as a two-dimensional being in a three-dimensional world. Amusingly illustrated by the author. 16 illustrations. 103pp. 5⅜ × 8½. 20001-9 Pa. $2.25

THE HISTORY OF THE LEWIS AND CLARK EXPEDITION, Meriwether Lewis and William Clark, edited by Elliott Coues. Classic edition of Lewis and Clark's day-by-day journals that later became the basis for U.S. claims to Oregon and the West. Accurate and invaluable geographical, botanical, biological, meteorological and anthropological material. Total of 1,508pp. 5⅜ × 8½.
21268-8, 21269-6, 21270-X Pa. Three-vol. set $26.85

LANGUAGE, TRUTH AND LOGIC, Alfred J. Ayer. Famous, clear introduction to Vienna, Cambridge schools of Logical Positivism. Role of philosophy, elimination of metaphysics, nature of analysis, etc. 160pp. 5⅜ × 8½. (Available in U.S. and Canada only) 20010-8 Pa. $2.95

MATHEMATICS FOR THE NONMATHEMATICIAN, Morris Kline. Detailed, college-level treatment of mathematics in cultural and historical context, with numerous exercises. For liberal arts students. Preface. Recommended Reading Lists. Tables. Index. Numerous black-and-white figures. xvi + 641pp. 5⅜ × 8½.
24823-2 Pa. $11.95

28 SCIENCE FICTION STORIES, H. G. Wells. Novels, *Star Begotten* and *Men Like Gods*, plus 26 short stories: "Empire of the Ants," "A Story of the Stone Age," "The Stolen Bacillus," "In the Abyss," etc. 915pp. 5⅜ × 8½. (Available in U.S. only)
20265-8 Cloth. $10.95

HANDBOOK OF PICTORIAL SYMBOLS, Rudolph Modley. 3,250 signs and symbols, many systems in full; official or heavy commercial use. Arranged by subject. Most in Pictorial Archive series. 143pp. 8⅜ × 11. 23357-X Pa. $6.95

INCIDENTS OF TRAVEL IN YUCATAN, John L. Stephens. Classic (1843) exploration of jungles of Yucatan, looking for evidences of Maya civilization. Travel adventures, Mexican and Indian culture, etc. Total of 669pp. 5⅜ × 8½.
20926-1, 20927-X Pa., Two-vol. set $9.90

DEGAS: An Intimate Portrait, Ambroise Vollard. Charming, anecdotal memoir by famous art dealer of one of the greatest 19th-century French painters. 14 black-and-white illustrations. Introduction by Harold L. Van Doren. 96pp. 5⅜ × 8½.
25131-4 Pa. $3.95

PERSONAL NARRATIVE OF A PILGRIMAGE TO ALMANDINAH AND MECCAH, Richard Burton. Great travel classic by remarkably colorful personality. Burton, disguised as a Moroccan, visited sacred shrines of Islam, narrowly escaping death. 47 illustrations. 959pp. 5⅜ × 8½. 21217-3, 21218-1 Pa., Two-vol. set $19.90

PHRASE AND WORD ORIGINS, A. H. Holt. Entertaining, reliable, modern study of more than 1,200 colorful words, phrases, origins and histories. Much unexpected information. 254pp. 5⅜ × 8½. 20758-7 Pa. $5.95

THE RED THUMB MARK, R. Austin Freeman. In this first Dr. Thorndyke case, the great scientific detective draws fascinating conclusions from the nature of a single fingerprint. Exciting story, authentic science. 320pp. 5⅜ × 8½. (Available in U.S. only) 25210-8 Pa. $5.95

AN EGYPTIAN HIEROGLYPHIC DICTIONARY, E. A. Wallis Budge. Monumental work containing about 25,000 words or terms that occur in texts ranging from 3000 B.C. to 600 A.D. Each entry consists of a transliteration of the word, the word in hieroglyphs, and the meaning in English. 1,314pp. 6⅞ × 10.
23615-3, 23616-1 Pa., Two-vol. set $31.90

THE COMPLEAT STRATEGYST: Being a Primer on the Theory of Games of Strategy, J. D. Williams. Highly entertaining classic describes, with many illustrated examples, how to select best strategies in conflict situations. Prefaces. Appendices. xvi + 268pp. 5⅜ × 8½. 25101-2 Pa. $5.95

THE ROAD TO OZ, L. Frank Baum. Dorothy meets the Shaggy Man, little Button-Bright and the Rainbow's beautiful daughter in this delightful trip to the magical Land of Oz. 272pp. 5⅜ × 8. 25208-6 Pa. $4.95

POINT AND LINE TO PLANE, Wassily Kandinsky. Seminal exposition of role of point, line, other elements in non-objective painting. Essential to understanding 20th-century art. 127 illustrations. 192pp. 6½ × 9¼. 23808-3 Pa. $4.95

LADY ANNA, Anthony Trollope. Moving chronicle of Countess Lovel's bitter struggle to win for herself and daughter Anna their rightful rank and fortune—perhaps at cost of sanity itself. 384pp. 5⅜ × 8½. 24669-8 Pa. $8.95

EGYPTIAN MAGIC, E. A. Wallis Budge. Sums up all that is known about magic in Ancient Egypt: the role of magic in controlling the gods, powerful amulets that warded off evil spirits, scarabs of immortality, use of wax images, formulas and spells, the secret name, much more. 253pp. 5⅜ × 8½. 22681-6 Pa. $4.50

THE DANCE OF SIVA, Ananda Coomaraswamy. Preeminent authority unfolds the vast metaphysic of India: the revelation of her art, conception of the universe, social organization, etc. 27 reproductions of art masterpieces. 192pp. 5⅜ × 8½.
24817-8 Pa. $5.95

CHRISTMAS CUSTOMS AND TRADITIONS, Clement A. Miles. Origin, evolution, significance of religious, secular practices. Caroling, gifts, yule logs, much more. Full, scholarly yet fascinating; non-sectarian. 400pp. 5⅜ × 8½.
23354-5 Pa. $6.50

THE HUMAN FIGURE IN MOTION, Eadweard Muybridge. More than 4,500 stopped-action photos, in action series, showing undraped men, women, children jumping, lying down, throwing, sitting, wrestling, carrying, etc. 390pp. 7⅞ × 10⅝.
20204-6 Cloth. $21.95

THE MAN WHO WAS THURSDAY, Gilbert Keith Chesterton. Witty, fast-paced novel about a club of anarchists in turn-of-the-century London. Brilliant social, religious, philosophical speculations. 128pp. 5⅜ × 8½. 25121-7 Pa. $3.95

A CEZANNE SKETCHBOOK: Figures, Portraits, Landscapes and Still Lifes, Paul Cezanne. Great artist experiments with tonal effects, light, mass, other qualities in over 100 drawings. A revealing view of developing master painter, precursor of Cubism. 102 black-and-white illustrations. 144pp. 8¾ × 6⅜. 24790-2 Pa. $5.95

AN ENCYCLOPEDIA OF BATTLES: Accounts of Over 1,560 Battles from 1479 B.C. to the Present, David Eggenberger. Presents essential details of every major battle in recorded history, from the first battle of Megiddo in 1479 B.C. to Grenada in 1984. List of Battle Maps. New Appendix covering the years 1967–1984. Index. 99 illustrations. 544pp. 6½ × 9¼. 24913-1 Pa. $14.95

AN ETYMOLOGICAL DICTIONARY OF MODERN ENGLISH, Ernest Weekley. Richest, fullest work, by foremost British lexicographer. Detailed word histories. Inexhaustible. Total of 856pp. 6½ × 9¼.
21873-2, 21874-0 Pa., Two-vol. set $17.00

WEBSTER'S AMERICAN MILITARY BIOGRAPHIES, edited by Robert McHenry. Over 1,000 figures who shaped 3 centuries of American military history. Detailed biographies of Nathan Hale, Douglas MacArthur, Mary Hallaren, others. Chronologies of engagements, more. Introduction. Addenda. 1,033 entries in alphabetical order. xi + 548pp. 6½ × 9¼. (Available in U.S. only)
24758-9 Pa. $11.95

LIFE IN ANCIENT EGYPT, Adolf Erman. Detailed older account, with much not in more recent books: domestic life, religion, magic, medicine, commerce, and whatever else needed for complete picture. Many illustrations. 597pp. 5⅜ × 8½.
22632-8 Pa. $8.95

HISTORIC COSTUME IN PICTURES, Braun & Schneider. Over 1,450 costumed figures shown, covering a wide variety of peoples: kings, emperors, nobles, priests, servants, soldiers, scholars, townsfolk, peasants, merchants, courtiers, cavaliers, and more. 256pp. 8⅜ × 11¼. 23150-X Pa. $8.95

THE NOTEBOOKS OF LEONARDO DA VINCI, edited by J. P. Richter. Extracts from manuscripts reveal great genius; on painting, sculpture, anatomy, sciences, geography, etc. Both Italian and English. 186 ms. pages reproduced, plus 500 additional drawings, including studies for *Last Supper, Sforza* monument, etc. 860pp. 7⅞ × 10¾. (Available in U.S. only) 22572-0, 22573-9 Pa., Two-vol. set $29.90

THE ART NOUVEAU STYLE BOOK OF ALPHONSE MUCHA: All 72 Plates from "Documents Decoratifs" in Original Color, Alphonse Mucha. Rare copyright-free design portfolio by high priest of Art Nouveau. Jewelry, wallpaper, stained glass, furniture, figure studies, plant and animal motifs, etc. Only complete one-volume edition. 80pp. 9⅜ × 12¼. 24044-4 Pa. $8.95

ANIMALS: 1,419 COPYRIGHT-FREE ILLUSTRATIONS OF MAMMALS, BIRDS, FISH, INSECTS, ETC., edited by Jim Harter. Clear wood engravings present, in extremely lifelike poses, over 1,000 species of animals. One of the most extensive pictorial sourcebooks of its kind. Captions. Index. 284pp. 9 × 12.
23766-4 Pa. $9.95

OBELISTS FLY HIGH, C. Daly King. Masterpiece of American detective fiction, long out of print, involves murder on a 1935 transcontinental flight—"a very thrilling story"—NY Times. Unabridged and unaltered republication of the edition published by William Collins Sons & Co. Ltd., London, 1935. 288pp. 5⅜ × 8½. (Available in U.S. only) 25036-9 Pa. $4.95

VICTORIAN AND EDWARDIAN FASHION: A Photographic Survey, Alison Gernsheim. First fashion history completely illustrated by contemporary photographs. Full text plus 235 photos, 1840–1914, in which many celebrities appear. 240pp. 6½ × 9¼. 24205-6 Pa. $6.95

THE ART OF THE FRENCH ILLUSTRATED BOOK, 1700–1914, Gordon N. Ray. Over 630 superb book illustrations by Fragonard, Delacroix, Daumier, Doré, Grandville, Manet, Mucha, Steinlen, Toulouse-Lautrec and many others. Preface. Introduction. 633 halftones. Indices of artists, authors & titles, binders and provenances. Appendices. Bibliography. 608pp. 8⅜ × 11¼. 25086-5 Pa. $24.95

THE WONDERFUL WIZARD OF OZ, L. Frank Baum. Facsimile in full color of America's finest children's classic. 143 illustrations by W. W. Denslow. 267pp. 5⅜ × 8½. 20691-2 Pa. $5.95

FRONTIERS OF MODERN PHYSICS: New Perspectives on Cosmology, Relativity, Black Holes and Extraterrestrial Intelligence, Tony Rothman, et al. For the intelligent layman. Subjects include: cosmological models of the universe; black holes; the neutrino; the search for extraterrestrial intelligence. Introduction. 46 black-and-white illustrations. 192pp. 5⅜ × 8½. 24587-X Pa. $6.95

THE FRIENDLY STARS, Martha Evans Martin & Donald Howard Menzel. Classic text marshalls the stars together in an engaging, non-technical survey, presenting them as sources of beauty in night sky. 23 illustrations. Foreword. 2 star charts. Index. 147pp. 5⅜ × 8½. 21099-5 Pa. $3.50

FADS AND FALLACIES IN THE NAME OF SCIENCE, Martin Gardner. Fair, witty appraisal of cranks, quacks, and quackeries of science and pseudoscience: hollow earth, Velikovsky, orgone energy, Dianetics, flying saucers, Bridey Murphy, food and medical fads, etc. Revised, expanded In the Name of Science. "A very able and even-tempered presentation."—The New Yorker. 363pp. 5⅜ × 8.
20394-8 Pa. $6.50

ANCIENT EGYPT: ITS CULTURE AND HISTORY, J. E Manchip White. From pre-dynastics through Ptolemies: society, history, political structure, religion, daily life, literature, cultural heritage. 48 plates. 217pp. 5⅜ × 8½. 22548-8 Pa. $5.95

SIR HARRY HOTSPUR OF HUMBLETHWAITE, Anthony Trollope. Incisive, unconventional psychological study of a conflict between a wealthy baronet, his idealistic daughter, and their scapegrace cousin. The 1870 novel in its first inexpensive edition in years. 250pp. 5⅜ʼ× 8½. 24953-0 Pa. $5.95

LASERS AND HOLOGRAPHY, Winston E. Kock. Sound introduction to burgeoning field, expanded (1981) for second edition. Wave patterns, coherence, lasers, diffraction, zone plates, properties of holograms, recent advances. 84 illustrations. 160pp. 5⅜ × 8¼. (Except in United Kingdom) 24041-X Pa. $3.50

INTRODUCTION TO ARTIFICIAL INTELLIGENCE: SECOND, EN-LARGED EDITION, Philip C. Jackson, Jr. Comprehensive survey of artificial intelligence—the study of how machines (computers) can be made to act intelligently. Includes introductory and advanced material. Extensive notes updating the main text. 132 black-and-white illustrations. 512pp. 5⅜ × 8½. 24864-X Pa. $8.95

HISTORY OF INDIAN AND INDONESIAN ART, Ananda K. Coomaraswamy. Over 400 illustrations illuminate classic study of Indian art from earliest Harappa finds to early 20th century. Provides philosophical, religious and social insights. 304pp. 6⅜ × 9⅜. 25005-9 Pa. $8.95

THE GOLEM, Gustav Meyrink. Most famous supernatural novel in modern European literature, set in Ghetto of Old Prague around 1890. Compelling story of mystical experiences, strange transformations, profound terror. 13 black-and-white illustrations. 224pp. 5⅜ × 8½. (Available in U.S. only) 25025-3 Pa. $6.95

ARMADALE, Wilkie Collins. Third great mystery novel by the author of *The Woman in White* and *The Moonstone*. Original magazine version with 40 illustrations. 597pp. 5⅜ × 8½. 23429-0 Pa. $9.95

PICTORIAL ENCYCLOPEDIA OF HISTORIC ARCHITECTURAL PLANS, DETAILS AND ELEMENTS: With 1,880 Line Drawings of Arches, Domes, Doorways, Facades, Gables, Windows, etc., John Theodore Haneman. Sourcebook of inspiration for architects, designers, others. Bibliography. Captions. 141pp. 9 × 12. 24605-1 Pa. $6.95

BENCHLEY LOST AND FOUND, Robert Benchley. Finest humor from early 30's, about pet peeves, child psychologists, post office and others. Mostly unavailable elsewhere. 73 illustrations by Peter Arno and others. 183pp. 5⅜ × 8½. 22410-4 Pa. $3.95

ERTÉ GRAPHICS, Erté. Collection of striking color graphics: *Seasons, Alphabet, Numerals, Aces* and *Precious Stones*. 50 plates, including 4 on covers. 48pp. 9⅜ × 12¼. 23580-7 Pa. $6.95

THE JOURNAL OF HENRY D. THOREAU, edited by Bradford Torrey, F. H. Allen. Complete reprinting of 14 volumes, 1837–61, over two million words; the sourcebooks for *Walden*, etc. Definitive. All original sketches, plus 75 photographs. 1,804pp. 8½ × 12¼. 20312-3, 20313-1 Cloth., Two-vol. set $80.00

CASTLES: THEIR CONSTRUCTION AND HISTORY, Sidney Toy. Traces castle development from ancient roots. Nearly 200 photographs and drawings illustrate moats, keeps, baileys, many other features. Caernarvon, Dover Castles, Hadrian's Wall, Tower of London, dozens more. 256pp. 5⅜ × 8¼.
24898-4 Pa. $5.95

AMERICAN CLIPPER SHIPS: 1833–1858, Octavius T. Howe & Frederick C. Matthews. Fully-illustrated, encyclopedic review of 352 clipper ships from the period of America's greatest maritime supremacy. Introduction. 109 halftones. 5 black-and-white line illustrations. Index. Total of 928pp. 5⅜ × 8½.
25115-2, 25116-0 Pa., Two-vol. set $17.90

TOWARDS A NEW ARCHITECTURE, Le Corbusier. Pioneering manifesto by great architect, near legendary founder of "International School." Technical and aesthetic theories, views on industry, economics, relation of form to function, "mass-production spirit," much more. Profusely illustrated. Unabridged translation of 13th French edition. Introduction by Frederick Etchells. 320pp. 6⅛ × 9¼. (Available in U.S. only)
25023-7 Pa. $8.95

THE BOOK OF KELLS, edited by Blanche Cirker. Inexpensive collection of 32 full-color, full-page plates from the greatest illuminated manuscript of the Middle Ages, painstakingly reproduced from rare facsimile edition. Publisher's Note. Captions. 32pp. 9⅜ × 12¼.
24345-1 Pa. $4.95

BEST SCIENCE FICTION STORIES OF H. G. WELLS, H. G. Wells. Full novel *The Invisible Man*, plus 17 short stories: "The Crystal Egg," "Aepyornis Island," "The Strange Orchid," etc. 303pp. 5⅜ × 8½. (Available in U.S. only)
21531-8 Pa. $6.95

AMERICAN SAILING SHIPS: Their Plans and History, Charles G. Davis. Photos, construction details of schooners, frigates, clippers, other sailcraft of 18th to early 20th centuries—plus entertaining discourse on design, rigging, nautical lore, much more. 137 black-and-white illustrations. 240pp. 6⅛ × 9¼.
24658-2 Pa. $6.95

ENTERTAINING MATHEMATICAL PUZZLES, Martin Gardner. Selection of author's favorite conundrums involving arithmetic, money, speed, etc., with lively commentary. Complete solutions. 112pp. 5⅜ × 8½.
25211-6 Pa. $2.95

THE WILL TO BELIEVE, HUMAN IMMORTALITY, William James. Two books bound together. Effect of irrational on logical, and arguments for human immortality. 402pp. 5⅜ × 8½.
20291-7 Pa. $7.50

THE HAUNTED MONASTERY and THE CHINESE MAZE MURDERS, Robert Van Gulik. 2 full novels by Van Gulik continue adventures of Judge Dee and his companions. An evil Taoist monastery, seemingly supernatural events; overgrown topiary maze that hides strange crimes. Set in 7th-century China. 27 illustrations. 328pp. 5⅜ × 8½.
23502-5 Pa. $5.95

CELEBRATED CASES OF JUDGE DEE (DEE GOONG AN), translated by Robert Van Gulik. Authentic 18th-century Chinese detective novel; Dee and associates solve three interlocked cases. Led to Van Gulik's own stories with same characters. Extensive introduction. 9 illustrations. 237pp. 5⅜ × 8½.
23337-5 Pa. $4.95

Prices subject to change without notice.
Available at your book dealer or write for free catalog to Dept. GI, Dover Publications, Inc., 31 East 2nd St., Mineola, N.Y. 11501. Dover publishes more than 175 books each year on science, elementary and advanced mathematics, biology, music, art, literary history, social sciences and other areas.